They Sleep In Trees

Elizabeth O Redbrook

A lot happened last summer. One of the twins disappeared and his brother and stepdad were lost without him. Mrs. Henley collapsed and died by her old pickup truck after a long, independent life. That's achieving a lot for someone who is only fourteen inches tall.

We live in an animal kingdom. Sometimes we look out onto the field and see deer, chickens, ducks, wild and domestic turkeys, birds, rabbits and squirrels mingling peacefully as they graze their morning snack. To the west, is more than seven thousand acres of protected swamp, creek and forest. It's a legally mandated animal sanctuary. For over ten years we have been able to watch and learn from them. Their world is changing all the time and we feel lucky to have been able to see the things we have. Each animal is both a unique individual and a certain type, just like most people. Imagine the stories they could tell if they could talk.

The animals are not protected for their own sakes. The world is ruled by humans. Animal needs are almost always secondary to human ones. Their land's true purpose is to protect the water that lies beneath. They are unknowing beneficiaries of living above a giant water farm which scrambles to fill the fast growing water demands of Tampa and the Gulf beaches. This unique location creates an opportunity for wildlife to flourish and, sometimes become a threat to domestic animals, because so many predators thrive there.

Free of confinement, chickens, ducks, turkeys, and even rabbits display a wide range of behaviors that can seem almost human. They are capable of forming families and having relationships that last a life time and they can also form lifelong rivalries and feuds. There are loners who isolate themselves, though most choose to live in small groups. Sometimes these, "families" form from all sizes, breeds and colors, while others associate only with others of their own "kind."

Once in a while a male and female form a singular bond and become a couple. They all have one thing in common; they are surrounded by constant danger. Those that survive need to be cautious, quick and lucky.

There are Only Two Kinds of Hens

By heritage, breed, size and temperament, there are dozens of types of chicken hens. There are fierce protectors of their chicks and those who appear virtually unaware they have them. They can be sweet natured, or screeching banshees. Hens propel their genes into the future, or die, by their egg laying habits.

Some hens seek the highest, most easily defended places to lay eggs and some, while they still seek cover, lay close to the ground. Here, at the edge of the great forest, that almost never works out. Also, while all hens lay eggs, some hens lay eggs and never sit on a nest, and some are perpetually sitting on any nest they can find.

We humans raised as we are with sacred notions of maternal instinct and mother's intuition, can judge some hen's to be either extremely cold, or we might attribute their actions to plain stupidity. That's a narrow view of habits that have allowed these birds to evolve through time and survive over many millennia. They have traveled from their ancestral homes, probably in India and other parts of western Asia, to every corner of the globe.

By the time of the early pharaohs they had made their way to Egypt. By the time of Plato, they had crossed the Mediterranean to

Europe. They have survived all manner of human interference and efforts to, "improve," everything about them. Despite all they have endured, they're population is higher than that of any other bird species, estimated at twenty four billion plus.

Hens lay eggs even if they've never seen a rooster in their life, they just don't become chicks. Lots of people who keep chickens for the eggs they lay don't keep roosters. This way they can avoid all the drama and noise they bring. But roosters and hens together play out the whole drama of life. Luckily, we have a little extra land, for roosters are much better behaved when they have room to roam. Lots of old timers think fertilized eggs taste better and are more nutritious as well. With roosters around, it's hard for hens to avoid their sexual attentions; they must be super fast and unafraid to hunker down under bushes or objects that can protect them from getting back jumped.

Hens that don't avoid roosters have fulfilled their biological function just by laying eggs. If she's not from a breed that's inclined to nest, someone else will do it for her. The wild chickens of the subcontinent, ancestors' of modern chickens, have a communal nesting policy. After many millennia of success, if it was good enough for them it's good enough for some of their great-granddaughters squared.

Aside from full blooded bantam hens and others that remain true to the ancient way of nesting low to the ground, most hens will lay their eggs in nest boxes or other high, protected enclosures provided for them. The others strike out on their own, hiding in bushes or in underbrush to make their nests. We live where we can go months and months without rain, or get ten inches in thirty six hours. The hens who seek out their own wild spots are experts at becoming nearly invisible in a spot where water won't puddle and destroy their eggs.

Chickens and turkeys despise being rained on and run for shelter after more than a light sprinkle, but ground nesting hens will

sit through days, or even weeks of rainstorms They keep their eggs warm and dry while they become thoroughly soaked.

When chickens are of more than one breed and size, community nesting makes it impossible to be absolutely sure of any individual chicks' parentage. Hens often don't seem to have the vaguest idea who their chicks are either. When we're replenishing a flock, we leave multiple eggs for the hens to hatch. If you don't fear getting attacked, it's easy to put several extra eggs in a nest. If a duck or turkey hatches out near the same time as the chicks, most hens will treat them exactly the same as a baby chick. This is almost always the case, even with hens don't get on well with grown ducks or turkeys. Sometimes none of the chicks look like the hen who kept them alive when they were inside their eggs.

Most sitting hens are pretty aggressive defenders of their nests. If you're putting eggs in, or taking some away, you're going to get attacked. One hen with a poor record of caring for live chicks had three sets of hatch offs in a row taken for their safety. This wasn't ninety days worth of sitting but only nine days as she was hatching eggs we had put there from other nests. The chicks generally hatch out one to four at a time, for one to two weeks in a shared or community nest.

After we had taken the third batch, she was pretty frustrated, for the next hen that had eggs hatch felt her wrath. She jumped off the nest and got all up in her face as if to say, "Oh no, if I don't get to keep mine, you don't get to keep yours." She didn't give her a minute's peace. When we corralled the mama hen and caught her chicks, she seemed satisfied. She hopped back up into her nest box to continue sitting.

Crow Chickens

Our chickens have been free to mix all sizes and breeds for almost ten years, so it's impossible to predict which hens will be nest sitters and which ones will lay eggs and leave someone else to do the actual work. One of the oddest phenomena to come from this free mixing of different breeds are those I call crow chickens. Of course, they're not actually crows, but in some ways resemble them.

They are about the size of small bantams, but without their grace and good looks. They are plain, beady eyed black hens who are fiercely clannish, often associating only with their own mothers and children, and occasionally mating with their own sons. Once a grandmother, mother and daughter were all that was left of what was once a clan of nine. They would come up on the porch every afternoon, demanding snacks and would even peck at your toes out in the yard if they didn't feel particularly well fed. They're not the only porch beggars we've had over the years, many of them are crows.

It is impossible to tell who the ancestors of these chickens are, for they have none of the characteristics of docile egg laying or good looks that humans normally breed chickens for.

Even after the floods we've had this summer, there is a near perfect nuclear, at least by their standards, crow family. Newborn chicks are nearly anonymous for several weeks. Some are black; some are pale yellow, which will become white, and some have a few marking feathers which will eventually give them beauty and distinction. But, essentially all black chicks look more or less alike as do all the yellow chicks except for colored markings. All their faces, eyes and expressions are similar. Their defining physical characteristics and unique behavioral traits come later. That makes it impossible to predict who will become a crow chicken, yet, at least one appears each season. No hen is more focused, attentive and persistent in protecting their family. They keep their little families together and slightly separate from other groups. As they age, a few little black chicks don't grow very tall. They're beady, yet expressive eyes are singularly focused. Keeping their family intact is their main job.

Hens are always disappearing and reappearing, though sometimes they disappear for good. Due to a hen's vulnerability while nesting, there is often an imbalance between the number of hens

and roosters, with the number advantage to the roosters. When an extra small crow chicken vanished early this rainy season, regrettably little notice was taken. The soggy ground and flooding creek brought other concerns. So, it was a cheerful spectacle one morning when the beady-eyed little lady marched up to the porch with two pairs of hatchlings. One pair was tiny and fully coal black and the other pair were, at first, only slightly larger. The larger pair had a few lighter feathers which offered the future promise of being able to guess at their possible parentage. Often you can see characteristics of any number of possible parents in the little ones as they grow. A crow chicken may look like an exact clone of its mother. The two smaller chicks looked as if they might, as they aged, become pure crow.

Crow chickens are the most attentive of mothers. Often, hens act as if their chicks are nothing but an annoyance, pecking around their feet and cheeping for attention. Often they wander off, leaving the chicks to keep up as best they can. These fearful females will leave their new born chicks helpless on the dangerous ground, as they go up to their preferred roosting spot at night. When this happens you must go, as it begins to grow dark, and round up the chicks and cage them for their own safety.

Mom never seems to miss them, and the next morning, she is happy to resume her group or her hen friends with nary a back word glance. Crow chickens are completely the opposite. They herd their chicks around with such discipline that a very young chick rarely gets more than a foot or two away from Mom, at least while they are very small. It helps that they are small and dark for they manage to hide themselves and their babies successfully night after night.

As Crow's babies grew, one of the smaller ones developed an unfortunately independent streak. She, for by now she had grown enough to tell, would try to wander away from the family and investigate things on her own. Any other time, this would be fine and normal, but this year we have not had normal circumstances. It began raining in mid-June and rained more than it has in one season, at least in our little corner of the world, in twenty years.

In 2005, the tropical storm / hurricane season brought one storm after another and Cypress Creek came up so far it flooded our woods, pines and pastures, higher than at any other time since we had lived here. But, the water receded very quickly and within a few days, all was more or less as it had been before. The only lasting physical damage was that our fishing hole was completely swallowed by the creek and all the fish vanished when it receded. The other damages are less visible to the naked eye. They mainly come out at night, for when the predators of the forest are flooded out of their usual hunting grounds, chickens are a very tempting alternative food source.

Orphan of the Storm

Flooded areas are a wonderland to predatory pond birds, as fish are washed from deep waters into temporary, shallow ponds and narrow pools. Aside from ducks, these appear to be the only animals that truly enjoy or benefit from floods. This summer, as high

ground became scarce, we were treated to a wonder-land of wild-life. Wild turkeys and groups of deer are so used to the sight of us that you can sometimes move to within a few feet of them without provoking flight. There is a dangerous side to all this beauty. Water moccasins are on the move as they seek higher ground and alligators often wander hundreds of feet from their normal swimming holes. Coyotes, foxes, raccoons, opossums and other predator mammals are also forced from their habitual territories into a shrinking area of dry ground.

For most of the time, every year, deer wander freely around our place. Despite hunting season, the deer population has grown, both in numbers and actual size, over the last decade. They have the seven thousand acres of preserve for their use, as well as zoning restrictions that limit building and additions along the creek, working in their favor. Deer, as a menace to society are nothing new to places in the north, but, here, deer in such robust numbers have not always been the norm. Now, they are so numerous, that as much as we love them, they will destroy roses, hibiscus and any other thing that strikes their fancy. Even the suburban neighborhoods surrounding us are not immune. The deer are bigger, tamer and more numerous than at any time in living memory.

The sad thing about the swelling deer population is the likelihood that some will be killed on the fast moving six lane highway less than a quarter mile from our house. One Thursday in June, we noticed a dead doe lying almost in the median of the highway just to the south of the convenience store/ car wash/ liquor store combo that was built at the end of the road a couple of years ago. There was a high probability that an adult doe that died in early summer might have left behind one or more baby deer, and she had.

That Saturday a fellow who lives down the street was walking to the store when he spied a brief splash of spotted color in the underbrush. It was a baby deer, seemingly, about a week old. He couldn't care for her and didn't have any experience with wildlife, so, he brought her to us. Deer often graze some distance from their newborns, so merely seeing one alone is no firm indication that they are orphaned. Still, this baby was only a few hundred feet from the run-over doe and she was lying, helpless close to two roads.

She was tiny and fragile. We prayed that she had at least a few days with her mother. If she hadn't, no amount of care could make-up for the antibodies and colostrums she needed from her mom. At night she would need a raised, secure enclosure to protect her tiny delicious looking body from predators, and, in the daytime she would need a secure larger enclosure where she could stretch her legs and grow. She would also need constant milk along with a slow but steady introduction to grasses, fruits, vegetables and vitamins. Plus she would need lots of nurturing as she was so alone in the world.

Raising a deer is nothing like raising a puppy, kitten or even a rabbit. Deer mothers are hands, more literally, tongues on. She will lick her baby all over, I mean, all over. This means that the babies need physical stimulation on a certain part of their bodies to, how shall I put this, complete the digestive process. When a human undertakes baby deer care, they must massage, with a cloth, just under the tale until they can go. Their digestion is especially delicate at the start of their lives, and failing to do this regularly, throughout the day, can be fatal to them. They can become dangerously backed up.

After a few weeks, this is no longer necessary, but at first, it was essential. We fed her goat milk and whole cow milk with a little half and half for extra calories. She loved her bottle and was always alert and ready to go from her little night enclosure to the larger, sunnier, covered, day time enclosure. At first my husband would carry her back and forth, but even tiny deer have extremely strong legs and sharp feet. Once she turned his side black and blue and ripped his shirt from kicking, it was time for a leash. The leash came at a fortunate time, for within a few days, it probably saved her life.

8

Right around two weeks after she came to live with us, Baby Deer experienced a major setback. When we went to give her a bottle that Sunday, she didn't want it, nor could she go to the bathroom. She walked to her pen rather listlessly and lay in the corner in a way that was not at all like her. She had something rather like colic. Massaging her tummy was one thing we had to do, and we had to keep her moving. Thank god for the leash, for she didn't feel like walking around on her own. My husband gave her baking soda solution in the kind of syringe you normally use to give dogs medicine.

Most of the time she walks along quietly sniffing at different plants and flowers and grasses, but then she does something strange. On a leash all of a sudden she would leap into the air, start suddenly and then land. That day she had not begun to leap yet, but was walking well, and thank God, showing some curiosity at the different smells she encountered on these walks. By the next morning she was beginning to return to normal and ate, not as heartily as usual, but well enough, and continued to improve as the day wore on. She is now several months' old and eating bananas, sweet potatoes, green peas, broccoli, carrots and grasses, along with feed corn. Her favorite food is, of course, the sweet, red new growth of Knock Out rose bushes. In the spring, when she will be old enough to free, I suspect someday none of the roses will be safe from her.

She is growing and doing well. Our son joked he was going to paint some fresh spots on her when she started the two month process of losing them. Like any proud and loving "parent," he sometimes wants to keep his little one frozen in time. But, lose her spots she did.

Her world is growing along with her. We started to let her come out of her fence and wander and jump around with us a couple of times a day. Like we all do, she needs exercise and what she used to get on a leash became dangerous for her and for us.

We used to hold the bottle up and as she craned her neck for it, we would slip the leash over her neck so she could take her exercise. As we weaned her we tried every other thing she liked, but, sweet potatoes, bananas, carrots and rose leaves were not enough of a delicacy for her to willingly let us place the leash over her neck. Her mighty, strong deer feet can hurt human skin pretty bad. A deer is a wild animal, so we only used the leash while she was very small.

We are letting her out to explore on her own. She can stretch her legs a little more and practice her leaping and then, so far so good, she returns to the sure goodies she knows will be waiting for her in her secure little haven. She is taking the baby steps we know she needs to take to join her free brethren soon when she is big enough, fast enough and strong enough.

At around five months we began letting her spend the day out, from slightly after sun up, to about an hour before dark. There are sometimes coyotes in the woods in the early evening, that's why we feel she should be in before it turns fully dark. We have to take our walks early, because one morning I let her out too early and we'd gotten several hundred feet before we realized she was following us. We led her back through the woods so she doesn't become familiar with the road.

Who's Your Daddy?

It's impossible to look at the baby chicks and figure out who their parents are in many cases. That's what makes their system so brilliant. Their genes can live on, even if they don't have a mother who hangs around through what must be the incredible boredom of sitting on a nest almost twenty four hours a day, for nearly a month.

Hatchery websites are a good place to research which breeds are sitters. If you just want eggs, you may not relish fighting the hen for them. We've let the breeds mix so over time they would become smaller, quicker and more maneuverable against predators, but, you can choose chickens for their egg size and color by doing a little reading.

Hens don't sit all the time and when they're free range and mixed breed, when and if they'll sit is impossible to predict.

We have wooden nest boxes mounted high on posts under the shed and around the chicken house, but, we've provided some roomier more creative nesting spaces as well. Dog crates, cat crates and an insulated type of doghouse called a Dogloo are other inexpensive options for nesting spaces. You can often find crates and dog houses at thrift stores, garage sales or on Craigslist. You have to elevate them at least four feet off the ground so they'll stay dry. Even with precautions taken, some egg eating, nest attacking predators aren't deterred by heights.

The Chick Magnets

It's a sad fact that in any given year, roosters will eventually outnumber hens by as much as four to one. Even when you compensate by buying more hen hatchlings, the numbers usually end up about the same, eventually. Observing hen behavior offers some clues to their high mortality rates. They are vulnerable when nesting, especially if they nest low to the ground, as turkeys and bantam hens do. Even those who nest in high dry nest boxes are vulnerable when their nearly month long, almost twenty-four hour a day sits, make them easy prey for raccoons, possums, owls and other night hunters. However, some hens never sit a nest and their numbers dwindle at almost the same rate. Two notable exceptions to the rule were hens that were "freed" by people who no longer wished to care for them and were coaxed onto our property by the need for feed. One was a red loner hen, seemingly middle aged when we found her grazing just past our mailbox. She was very tame and docile, and literally followed us home. Our daughter named her Henley, which eventually became Mrs. Henley.

She was a big hen. She was too large to roost easily in the trees and she was afraid of a strange hen house, so we put a little shelter on the picnic table to give her at least a little protection from the owls and other night predators. This suited her just fine and though she always preferred her own company, when we got more chickens, she got along pretty well with everyone. Toward the end of her life, she began hanging around with a couple of other "mature" hens. They would wander around pecking and clucking, no doubt gossiping about the suspect behavior of all the young folk. More about her adventures later.

Our other most enduring drop-offs were a group of five sisters, or so we assumed. They were so similar it was hard to tell one from the other. They were not much to look at, small and thin with hawk like noses, beady little eyes and pale, brownish-red feathers. They had the look of some wild game, type bird as much as they resembled chickens. We ended up calling them the Chanel Five. We spied them pecking along the side of the road, it wasn't hard to herd them back to the property with arm waving and the golf cart. It was months before they would associate with anyone out of their sisterhood. The similarity between these hens and Mrs. Henley was that they all had very long and peaceful lives. But, this is not the norm.

Some hens don't get killed while they are nesting, some are captured while roosting or just wandering around oblivious to their surroundings. Henley lived a long life by keeping close to the house. The Chanel sisters survived by being very aware of their surroundings. As essential as this awareness is to the survival of small vulnerable birds, few hens seem capable of being careful or observant of the places they want to forage. They will wander right up to the edge of the woods, or into thick snaky bushes oblivious to the danger. This is where good roosters come in.

The most important job for a rooster, aside from fertilizing as many different hens' eggs as he can, is being the sentry that keeps watch, while the hens graze to their hearts content. We've had a number of good roosters over the years, but consistently some of the most popular with the hens are the Turken Men. Turken's aren't part turkey, they just look like they are, because, like turkeys, they have naked necks and faces with feathers so fine that they almost look like skin. They come in a wide range of reds, gold, greens and every other color found in the chicken spectrum. The ladies just love these guys because, they defend their hens from the attentions of rogue males, and more importantly, they are the best security guards, against predators in the business.

The best we ever had were two Turkens who were hatched out here on our place. The brothers stayed as thick as thieves for about nine months as they grew stronger and more confident. They were absolutely stunning, and so close that they were endearing to watch. Like most young roosters, the only sex for them was to be had through sexual assault. Hens just don't gravitate voluntarily to young cocks. Unless they are growing up in a family, or an orphan group that is thrown together for mutual security, hens and roosters don't as a rule associate very much when they're very young. Roosters only attract hens once they're fully grown, between nine months to a year old.

When they came of age, the brothers split up for good, yet each managed to acquire large and diverse harems. To the untrained eye it might seem that they were popular because they were good-sized, but not over large, good-looking boys. That wasn't it; looks mean absolutely nothing to chickens. They were formidable fighters when challenged, though they seldom were.

Roosters flailing up ruffling their feathers and kicking their feet is impressive to see and often done to show off for the ladies. As I said, they didn't fight much, they didn't need to. Their popularity probably came from the fact that hens felt absolutely safe and guarded twenty-four / seven when they were with them. A good rooster doesn't eat much while the hens are eating, they are almost perpetually turning 360 degrees both their bodies, and circling around the hens. There is about two acres of fairly open field between the pine grove and the forest. Part of it used to be pines, but all the pines have died and most of the palms, loquats and bottlebrush we've planted over the years have not become terribly thick.

It's the most dangerous of habitats, open field next to a preda-tor filled forest. Early mornings, before the sun has scorched the dew off the grass, there must be a lot of bugs out there to eat. When the guard rooster sees anything suspicious he makes a loud noise, which is not quite a crow, and the flock flees back to the safety of the

backyard or chicken yard .They make a very loud and fearful noise as they go, but it's not long before they brave the scene again. The bravest roosters either circle the foraging flock, or march back and forth between them and the point where an attack is most likely to come from.

Jilted Romeo

We have some pretty roosters this year, three I especially liked, remind me of cavaliers, with a comb like a tri-cornered hat and long fine blonde feathers around their necks, that look like a long shag haircut. Their body feathers are black and white, or spotted. We were favored with a small, medium and large version of this rooster.

Since a large group of chicks had been raised together, freely able to choose their own friends, like with humans, clicks formed. As they grew to maturity these three roosters, a large Rhode Island Red rooster, a black one and two white roosters with spots on their tales hung out together. This "gang" spent all their time together, along with two large pretty white hens. This was the way they wanted it, and since they favored spending most of their time in the yard or in the flower beds, probably so they can scarf up Baby Deer's leftover veggies and corn, they seemed as if they would be pretty safe. As luck would have it, one of the pretty hens went missing, despite the fact that she went willingly into the henhouse to be locked up every night.

I scratched my head at one hen keeping company with seven roosters, because even though I never saw them jumping her, they were certainly getting old enough. I saw many of the smaller roosters of the same age chasing hens around all the time.

One evening I saw the larger cavalier, as I called him, and the pretty white hen break away from the rest of the group and head out to roost in the opposite direction from their friends. They headed over to an ancient oak tree, by the shed, and hopped up on our old farm tractor. I went to the deck rail to see this unexpected show. I was sure that the hen would have a very difficult time hopping up from the tractor seat, or hood ,into the branches, because she was a fairly large, wide breasted chicken. The rooster was smaller boned and wiry, though he was slightly taller than she was.

He leapt easily into the dense branches. Instinct had led him away from the noisy crowded chicken house to the best natural night protection, dense, leafy branches. The huge, spreading oak by the chicken house, long favored by the older chickens, was going through a leaf shedding faze, perhaps that accounted for their change of scene. Another possible answer is that as very young chickens they may have felt they would have a hard time establishing a place in the "pecking order" among the older more established birds. Pretty White Hen persevered, and within several minutes she was safely up in the branches where it would be an easy climb to a dense leafy roost. I watched them go through this evening ritual for the next month. They appeared to have formed that rarest of things in birds, or humans, a happy monogamous couple. The way it looked, this guy only had one weakness in keeping his lady friend. He's a little too early to bed, and she likes to stay up later.

The other evening I caught her other steady suitor, the handsome black rooster, chasing her around the car. He caught her pretty quick and hopped on top of her without any challenge from the other guy. I got worried that something had happened to her steady fellow. I went to the tree by the tractor and looked up and there he was. He clearly could see what happened, but guarding her all day was exhausting and he looked too sleepy to fly out of the tree and administer rooster justice.

About this time I noticed that while the seemingly happy couple still mingled with their old gang most of the day, she was starting to wander from the group more than she had. When she did, one of the new Turken boys always seemed to be close by. She continued to goof around the yard in the evening with her fellow, for another week and a few days, but the break-up was already easy to spot. He had just

failed to behave in a properly jealous, "This is my woman," attitude she seemed to expect in this situation. I'm sure the Turken expected to be challenged when he became a little too forward with the lady, but, I never saw it happen.

Even though chickens are not usually prone to violence, displays of aggression are common in these situations. When Mr. Chanticleer failed to stand up for his lady and demand the Turken cease and desist, she seemed to lose all faith in her man and her old gang.

One morning she was missing from her old gang. She was about fifty feet away with the Turken, who was clearly determined to keep her away from the tempting whiles of any other rooster. She seemed clearly captivated by his singular attention. She'd hop up on the golf cart and ruffle her feathers seductively at her assembled abandoned boys as if to say, "Look at what you gave up." She'd hop up on the bricks around the flower beds and stretch out, one leg and then another, as her new man stands enthralled with his good luck.

She was lucky, there were few females around, because he was clearly the type of guy that can attract a large number of girls. When they were moving through a crowd, he'd weave around her in a figure 8 and maintain a barrier of at least five feet between her and any other potential rival who might jump her unexpectedly.

Even the strictest of bodyguards must rest occasionally. One afternoon after it rained, Turken Man, Pretty White Hen and one of her former suitors sat comfortably and shared the arms of a lawn chair while they dried themselves off. Still, this was a rare instance of non-strategic relaxation. He knows if she left one rooster, she can leave another.

The three cavaliers were always together. One morning several days after Pretty White Hen left, her first beau, he was missing . I looked all over, but he wasn't with any of the usual suspects. While the timing may have just seemed suspicious, it seemed as if he may have wandered off and been so distracted by his newly single status that his usual survival instinct may have been damaged to a degree that became fatal. Now I only have one gallant cavalier of the original three left but, so far, he is hanging in there.

The Maybe Merry Widow

So far, so good, for Pretty White Hen and the Turken Man seemed to have a happy marriage, or whatever chickens have. Except for the few times of day when they desired the company of other animals, they spent all of their time alone. Except for those times in the evening when his exhaustion from watching over his highly desirable hen catches up with him, his efficient methods of surveillance and separation kept her quite safe from the attention of other roosters. Yet, in the evenings I would still see her lingering around Baby Deer's pen waiting for some spilled vegetables or a little extra corn. The big black rooster would always be there, and while I sought to respect their privacy, more than once I saw the familiar sexual commerce that I had seen that first night, her first rooster went to bed early. It would be almost dark before she would break away from her evening friends and go to the oak tree in the opposite direction from the path

the Black Rooster took towards his chicken house. He was too big to be able to roost easily in the trees.

Weeks went by, Turken Man though early to bed, was also early to rise. They would hang around for breakfast vegetables and then make their rounds of the property together and alone, showing up only for the social, dusting-napping hours during the heat of the day. This is rather like human cocktail hour.

Dusting is the way chickens clean themselves. They find a clean sandy spot and scratch and shake their way clean for about ten to twenty minutes. Often the effort seems to make them sleepy and some of them will seem to doze afterward. Their flight response is still very strong, so they aren't fully asleep. They went their separate ways from the others again, but then made friendly during other rigidly scheduled times of the day. If things had stayed the same, I can only wonder if they would have become one of the enduring romances of the chicken world. But, it was not to be.

A couple of months later I noticed Pretty White Hen wandering about by herself as if her previously poised, super model self suddenly did not know what to do. This was big news in our tiny little chicken world. It was as if all of a sudden Angelina began showing up in paparazzi pictures all alone and no one knew where Brad was. It was as if he had fallen off the face of the earth. It was several days before I could accept the truth. Even though exhaustive searches of all the places that were on his daily route showed no tell tale signs of feathers, I had to admit to myself that he was probably gone forever.

She makes a gallant little figure. After two seemingly happy, mainly monogamous relationships, Pretty White Hen seems in no hurry to enter into any kind of permanent relationship anytime soon. In fact, being a widow seems, in some ways to have widened her horizons. Instead of seeking out the next guy, or as her history has shown at times, a gang of guys, she has broadened her scope of friends. She now spends part of her day clucking and gossiping under the bushes with some of the other unattached hens. I will have to follow her in the evening to see if she has introduced any of her new friends to her old roosting place by the tractor. I still see her going there to roost. Once a chicken feels the freedom of sleeping in the trees they never go back to the hot, dark chicken houses unless they become too old to fly and climb.

Little Chicken Big World

My favorite breeds of chickens are the little fellows, bantams or bantys as we call them. The loveliest hen I think we ever had was little French White or Mrs. French White as I called her. We have some new buff or golden tan ones and ones who are buff with black tails, some who are white and white with black tails. Most of them are very small, but due to crossbreeding we have some bigger bantam crosses too. One of the all white roosters is beginning to acquire a steady harem. He will shepherd as many as five hens around the place. He has two regular "wives."

One of them has dots on the feathers on the back of her head that look just like a smiley face. Both his hens are a little bigger than he is. It's a lot easier for a rooster to breed bigger hens, than for big roosters to breed little hens, even though they try.

A very big rooster and a very small hen can breed successfully, but only with a lot of protest on the hen's part. Some of those guys are just way too big for them. Some of the most beautiful birds are the products of what is called out-crossing. You can get a rainbow of colors and a nice mix of sizes. Anybody who has ever had a mixed breed dog can tell you mixed breeds tend to be smarter and more adaptable than pure breeds. There has been a disturbing development in purebred chickens in the last few years. Some of them seem to have grown dangerously stupid.

One of the first things we learned in the attempt to successfully bring our hens and roosters from across the road was the need to outcross them to improve their survival skills. We had the most beautiful purebred chickens, the biggest strongest Homburgs, Fayoumis.

Domenickers, Rhode Island Reds, White Rocks and some other assorted ones when we moved here. They had a big safe barn to roost in and thousands of acres to roam at will, what could go wrong?

Gimme Shelter

A lot. One of the problems with the blank slate we had acquired was a lack of shelter for the birds. Anything will do for hens to dart under when avoiding the male's attentions, or for all of them to shield themselves from predator birds. We just didn't have much yet, except for under the cars or under the porch. Lawn chairs and a cedar picnic table, we found abandoned on the road, were a big help, but the flowers and trees we planted would need time to grow. At night there was a big sheet metal barn for them though.

Every morning when we opened the barn door they would have to scurry across an open field for at least 200 feet before they could seek the partial refuge of the pines. It didn't take long before they started getting picked off. These guys were flat dumb, at least where survival instincts factored in.

In many ways, I think animals are like fruits and vegetables after thousands of years of human manipulation. You may have noticed that most tomatoes you buy in the store last longer than they used to, but are tougher and less delicious than they used to be. As a former farmer I know a little bit about this. The perfectly natural desire to have vegetables that last longer with fewer losses to rotting always comes with a price.

One simply cannot breed one characteristic into anything without altering and modifying something else. The same thing has happened often in citrus breeding. The most delicious and by far the juiciest lemon is the Meyer's, but it comes with several flaws. They must be clipped from the tree, which is far more time consuming and labor intensive than picking. Their worst feature is a lovely, though thin and easily bruisable skin.

Shifting weather patterns made Central Florida more prone to hard winters in the 80's and 90's. This drove a quest to develop a cold hardy juice orange that would rival the yield and quality of Hamlins and Valencias. This led to what everyone believed to be a breakthrough. The new tree was called the Amber Sweet. It was a vigorous, fast growing tree and had a juicy attractive fruit. The publicity surrounding their introduction had caused people to ask for them, so we planted about fifty trees and waited till the winter to see what they would taste like.

When the verdict came in, they were guilty of being just about the blandest tasting thing ever. They tasted like water with a tiny bit of sugar in it. We thought they were just awful. We didn't have it as bad as some of the big groves that sold to juice plants though. Some people did actually like them, but that isn't how juice plants buy fruit. Fruit is graded by two standards, one of beauty, with those with the best shape, skin and color given the highest grade, and usually reserved for sale as fresh fruit. The other standard is called the solids test, but really tells how much sweetness is in the fruit. The density of the solids, or pulp, as most people call it, is tested and fruit with higher solids fetches a higher price than those with low solids. Amber Sweets had such a low density of solids, that the same amount of acreage that would have previously supported a family, or even made a small fortune, were now only bringing, literally pennies, or at the most dimes, on the dollars they had yielded before. Almost overnight, thousands of acres of land went on the market and fueled the suburban population explosion in Pasco, Hernando and south Hillsborough counties. The effects of this phenomenon are still with us today.

A Rose by any Other Name

If you like roses and have observed them over time, you know the roses of today are vastly different from their wild ancestors. The original roses were often single petalled and bloomed only once a

year. All old roses had unique and wonderful smells that impressed everyone, even though they didn't look like what we think of as roses. Over centuries of selective breeding, roses were first given the wonderful trait of repeat blooming. More colors were bred and by the late eighteenth century, most new varieties were colorful, multi-petalled and sweet smelling. By the late nineteenth century, tea roses married the best traits of all its ancestors. This might have been a good place to stop, but you know humans, if we can change it, we will, even when we shouldn't.

The twentieth century brought a perfect storm of genetic manipulation. Floribundas, Grandifloras, and Hybrid Teas were bigger and had more layers of petal than roses ever had before, but, again, one good thing brings a change in other desirable things. Everybody that has ever instinctively lowered their head to smell from a rose bouquet, knows that many of today's roses while beautiful and colorful, have scents ranging from mild, to pleasant, but hardly intoxicating. This can be remedied by buying some antique roses to plant among their supermodel descendents. Then you can have the scent and the maximum show.

Believe me, chickens over the several thousand years they have lived with humans, have been manipulated as much as roses or crops, maybe more. Throughout history, people have made them, bigger, smaller, bred them for bigger eggs, colored eggs and any other number of crazy or clever things we have wanted them to be able to do. In many ways this has been a good thing, for the chicken has benefitted in food and security from some of its' human associations, and God knows we have benefitted from them. We have made them bigger, smaller, prettier, more colorful, more hostile, or more docile, depending on our needs.

I have mentioned the tendency we have observed that there are usually far more roosters than hens, because the hens are more vulnerable. Fresh eggs are much better than store bought ones. Last March we bought twenty five hens of an improved laying variety.

They had a little bit of a game look about them though, and we hoped they would help them be more intelligent. They're a variety that is noted for the size and flavor of their eggs. We secured a fenced area, put a tin and shingled house in it and secured the bottom, to keep predators from digging in. We did this with laminated political signs and ceramic tile. They had a perfectly clean, safe place, with plenty of room to grow.

When we picked them up and brought them home, they were fine for a while, until they were old enough to be let out into a bigger yard in the day time. Those poor little things could find more ways to get killed, than I have ever seen that number of chickens do before.

We also noticed another very peculiar thing. Most chickens stay very calm around humans, or anything they are used to seeing all the time. These girls were completely the opposite. Normally, all you have to do to get chickens or turkeys to go into their houses at night, is to stand behind them, kind of wave your arms and walk toward the house saying something soothing or you can shout, it usually doesn't matter. Oh no, not with these girls. They would fly up in my face, fly into the fence or run around the yard screaming in terror. I had never seen chickens who behaved this way in my life. This was especially strange since we had tended to them since they were several days old. Usually familiarity and the fact that you are their food provider produces extra docility.

When they were two months old, we still had twenty-five. They were soon going to drop like flies. Some of the deaths were explainable; we had put one pretty feather-footed chicken with unusual ruffled and twisted feathers into the pen with them. She could have company where there was a lot of grass that would help keep her feathers clean. She roosted a little too close to the fence one night and in the morning, there was her sweet, feathered little body pulled half way through the wire. We moved the roosting poles toward the center of the enclosure. Over the next few weeks three more little chickens ended up dead inside the pen, all unexplained. I found them

when I would go let them out in the morning. Still, we would have had plenty of white hens to make eggs, if the numbers had stayed the same. Sometimes there is nothing you can do. You rack your brain wondering what you could have done, or where you might have moved them, but there is no point to it. Sometimes it's just the way of nature. Some survive, but they must be quick, wary and above all lucky. The peculiar way these little hens reacted to my attempts to keep them safe was, perhaps a clue to what would happen to most of them eventually.

Our exhaustive attempts to put them up at night were indeed, exhausting. Sometimes we would take turns and sometimes we would try to fan out and put them up as a team. They were truly destructive. The way their yard had been built left a little open lane beside the chicken house about three feet wide and eight feet long. This was their preferred escape route. Of course when we left their door open a few inches and shooed them in we got, usually, all but three or four of them. As we herded the rest of them back to the door, the ones inside would fly out and run quickly back the thirty feet or so, all the way to the gate. Well, we like to think that we didn't fall off of a turnip truck yesterday. First we tacked up our trusty old political signs to block the tunnel, but they tore them down. For a few days, we just patiently budgeted a little time to tack the signs back up. Then one evening when we went to lock them up, we saw that they had totally shredded weatherproof laminated signs that normally would have lasted for years. Now chickens can be vandals the same way that human can, but something reasonably solid is generally too much of a challenge for them to mess with.

Their favorite medium to vandalize is Styrofoam. When someone left a Styrofoam cooler in the back of our old red Ford F-150, some days later I wondered what the small white snow like flakes were that kept flying about. The chickens had pecked the cooler into a million tiny bits. A convenience store coffee cup that might blow onto the property, a Styrofoam to-go container, or a carelessly discarded lot of packing peanuts would face the same fate. Of course, we are always ordering things online, but we try to take all the Styrofoam packing peanuts and save them until we're potting plants. You mix it with the lower soil and it helps the drainage. The other thing that they destroy, is actually good for the earth, but costs us a lot of extra labor.

We mulch the dozen or so flower beds we have, usually twice a year. We don't spend any money, we use leaves, or pine needles, or, for the most visible beds right by the house, the bark that sheds off the dead pine trees, which looks just like expensive pine bark mulch. Around here, all you have to do is gather the dead bark, spray it with some bleach-water and it makes a safe, free alternative to the paper mill waste sold for several dollars a bag in the stores. Chickens have been engineered to break down this refuse of nature by their incessant scratching.

Few things are prettier than a freshly mulched flower bed. Chickens will let you enjoy the fruits of your labor for a while. Eventually their natural tendency to scratch, as they hunt for bugs catches up with your best gardening intentions. As with most things, their scratching brings a benefit as well as a bother. For as they churn, turn and destroy, mulch, leaves and sticks, they are also adding exponentially to the topsoil. Topsoil loss is a major environmental hazard. So, just because they make you want to shoot little pellet guns at them when they are tearing up your landscaping, doesn't mean that they aren't being good stewards of the earth.

Dealing with these kids on a day to day basis is a good lesson in what is and isn't biodegradable, even if you didn't already know. Once, for a while we were picking up containers full of school leftovers to feed the animals. We would do our best to get rid of the plastic utensils, condiment packs, and disposable yogurt containers, but sometimes they would get away from us. Even in the rankest most destructive mud we had seen in twenty years, none of this stuff would do more than just lay there, resisting the best efforts of our little topsoil builders. But that is one of the major reasons that it has

been years since I have used disposable packaging, or very much in the way of non-recycled packaging, except for one or two garbage bags a week.

Off the lecture desk and back to my story, sometimes even the smartest birds with the best instincts get killed. Older birds that have the same kind of joint and muscle aches as we do can be in danger, as they are unable to roost high enough in the trees for camouflage, which for them equals safety. Even the wisest old birds can get picked off when they hurt too much to climb high in the trees. They sometimes seem too proud to go into a chicken house with those they perhaps perceive as wimpy losers. They are creatures of habit and resist changing their roosting spot, unless they have been threatened. By then, it may be too late. Then there are the suicidal and stupid ones.

Of all the chickens we have ever seen who can exhibit stupid behavior and all breeds are susceptible to this, a pure bred Aracuana will exhibit far more stupidity than almost any other breed. What nature doesn't provide in the way of biology, organisms will often learn to compensate for. If they don't, we probably won't be seeing them anymore.

Aracuana chickens have biologically acquired a behind that has no butt to speak of. This may have happened slowly, probably after many generations. It could also be the result of a random mutation. The up side of this was big fast chickens, that were built in such a clever way that it was almost impossible for slower predators to run up behind them and grab them by their tail feathers. They don't have any tail feathers. The yin and yang kicked in again probably after many generations, because the ability to elude prey with speed and biology once again brought an unintended consequence. They sometimes appear to be the stupidest of all poultry, rivaling even domestic turkeys.

Perhaps the extra added ability to lay large numbers of good size eggs has been the reason that these poor chickens have lived as long as they do. Humans may have saved them. In our experience they often lived short lives and were wiped out in large numbers. It is never a pleasant thing to go down in the morning, to feed and let them out, and find a dead one inside. Some of the others will peck at it and eat the flesh, as they do with any meat.

Poultry like meat and a certain amount of protein is good and necessary for them, especially when they are little. We often give chicks and ducks ground, dry dog food, or cat food, to promote faster growth and healthy bones when chicks are young. If you throw down a bit of burger, fish or chicken, watch how fast they will come after it.

When we were getting the school leftovers, the last thing the birds would eat is the things we feed them, like grains, fruits and vegetables. They prefer the same stuff that most Americans do, burgers, pizza, pasta, and fries. One of the things we have in common.

But, I digress, the point is we had never lost so many chickens so quickly as we began to do with these hens. By the time they were down to a dozen we decided that since they were big enough and they weren't being afforded any special protection from being in a fence, not to mention the fact that they were so hard to put in at night, in the morning we would let them go.

I walked behind them pushing them towards their first taste of the big world. Some of them seemed reluctant to leave the only place they could remember, but, within a few minutes they seemed to be enjoying themselves, scratching up tender grass out in the field. Clearly, two cliques had formed. One group favored the left side of the fence and worked their way up and down it several times daily, while a little less than half of the other ones favored the right side. They identically mirrored the movements of the others, going up and down along the fence.

For the first several days, all went as well as could be hoped for. The count of both groups showed the same numbers as had left the fence a few days before. They also followed the older birds into one of the houses in the evening without protest. Maybe being free and seeing the behavior of older, smarter birds was having a good effect

on the girls. They mixed with the other groups, hesitantly at first, but so far so good. In another week, all hell would break loose for them. Then they started to die off, one by one and even two would be vanished on some days.

Within several weeks, there were only four. We won't be getting many eggs from this group. The remaining four will do better though. They have fully integrated into an adult group and eat and nest with their elders and hopefully receive some knowledge and protection from them. They are not very bright, but chickens are never loved for their brains.

Not Quite the Garden of Eden

Even educated, well informed people frequently have perceptions of the world that are so strong, that facts notwithstanding, are firmly and unshakably believed. Most people have heard the Everglades referred to as, "the River of Grass," as I had. But, even though I knew the venerable wetland was a wide expanse of navigable, saw grass, I always held an unshakable belief that it was surrounded by a jungle, or at least a lot of trees.

I was literally shocked when I first saw it as an adult. The same disconnect happens to people whose perceptions of Florida have been shaped by television and movies. They are often shocked, really shocked that all of Florida doesn't look like Miami on *Burn Notice*.

Florida is not really a land of soft palms blowing in a gentle breeze. Most of the trees people associate with their fantasy images of Florida actually have been imported from the islands of the South Pacific, or the rainforests of South America. Aside from the beaches, which often were not originally white sand, and the mangrove barriers, much of Florida looks like some of the rest of the southeastern United States. In other words, land like you see in the movie *the Yearling*.

There are basically four kinds of land in Florida, high, sandy ground typically covered with pine and palmetto. This is the land of the Eastern Diamondback Rattlesnake. It also comes as a great surprise to many folks that there is so much grazing land here.

For decades there were more small cattle ranches, and more young cattle, in Florida than any other state in the US. The third type of land is the reasonably fertile oak, maple and other deciduous type forest.

The fourth type comprises a very large portion of the state. These are the true wetlands and cypress swamps. These are often the home of our other terrifying neighbor, the Cottonmouth Water Moccasin. Unfortunately, he also lives in the oak woods on territory he sometimes shares with the rattlesnakes and the legendary red and yellow kill a fellow, Coral Snakes, who can also kill you.

The desires of nineteenth century railroad and real estate tycoons, to reshape the natural landscape in their own image, has influenced our modern desire to do the same.

When we bought this piece of property, it had all four types of land in miniature. There was swamp, oak, pasture and high sandy pine. There was also a lot of clean up to do, but basically we were blessed with a blank canvas we could paint as we wished. The first three bushes I planted, before we even moved here, were plumbagos, very popular thick, bushes with blue flowers. These could grow without much water. Lots of people don't realize how fragile many plants they associate with Florida are when first planted. Easy to kill if they are not watered continuously, especially in the heat.

We used to own a plant nursery. One day we were driving through a nearby neighborhood and noticed two expensive plants we had sold, shriveling on a hot driveway, still in their black, plastic pots. Obviously they hadn't been watered. At least the young couple who bought them didn't demand their money back, like some people would have. Still they came in about a week later, perplexed and curious as to why their new plants were dying.

Since we bought this place in 1996, we have planted hundreds of trees and flowers. Except in the dead of winter when only roses and a few other flowers are still blooming, we have every color in one season or another. As most of us do, we have tried to mold the land into our vision of beauty, but for the most part, we respect, and try to be good stewards of the land we live on.

I'm very proud of the fact that so many of the beautiful plants we enjoy every day are salvage other people discarded or gave up on. Even though some plants freeze to the ground almost every winter, people from up north often don't realize that if they cut the plants back in early spring, the plants will grow back quickly. Rates of growth for many tropical and semi-tropical plants are often as fast as four to ten inches a week. We have one type of plant that is so prolific that it has almost become a nuisance.

We bought one candle bush at a nursery about five years ago. It's pretty most of the year, but especially in the early fall when it puts on a yellow flower that resembles an iridescent, yellow candle. From one plant we now have several hundred. Most of them have spread on their own from the only unattractive thing about them, the large multi-pronged black seed pods that open to reveal several dozen seeds in each one. These are true tropicals that freeze to the ground every year and grow ten feet tall by mid- summer. They grow wider with age as the centers die out and then the next year's shoots grow up around them. There is one at Busch Gardens that is about fifteen feet across. My back garden is almost entirely filled with other people's failed gardening projects. Being that we live on a little used road, we are sometimes the unwilling beneficiaries of people's tree trimmings and sometimes, plants they have pulled up thinking they are dead. We have gained white birds of paradise, bougainvillea. Angel trumpets philodendrons, ferns, bananas, palms, gingers and yellow cassia trees this way. There is a ten foot or so section of purple flowers growing along the side of the road. They are ones we see for sale in nurseries and stores. Obviously someone threw some yard clippings there and they "volunteered" as we call it. There's several bushes of bleeding hearts around the corner that probably got there the same way.

We have a vine that grows along the side of the road, clearly something that someone brought from the north, for it identical to a lavender aster. I liked the color so much my husband rooted some for me. There are sometimes jasmines and honeysuckles along some roads, that can be rooted too.

Sometimes people don't want to take big, heavy, potted plants when they move. Sometimes they give them away, or sell them very cheaply. We gained a number of plants from Thailand when we bought a house from a lady that collected them. We gained some yellow and orange flowering trees that we had never had before this way.

The third way might sound a little weird, but I may as well confess that we are not against doing a little dumpster diving to supplement our plant collection. Some stores like Wal-Mart and Home Depot, have such a sweet deal with their suppliers that they just send back the dead plants and the suppliers come and pick them up. Some stores try clearance first, and then just throw away the ones they can't sell. My husband, or our handy man have found behind stores, or in dumpsters, roses, peach, red and pink hibiscus, jasmine vines, dozens of annuals and butterfly bushes. So, don't be afraid to look, free plants are out there. You just have to know where to look for them.

These Trees Can Kill You

Death is part of the circle of life. Something or someone, is dying around us all the time, we just don't like to think about it. That's a hard thing to ignore around here. When we moved here, in 2001, all of the pines on the property looked healthy and intact. Around four years later, they were attacked by pine borers. You could literally hear them inside the trees, separating the outer bark from the interiors. For the last few years we have had to schedule a fair amount of time

for picking up fallen branches, picking peeled bark off the ground and sawing down and hauling off the trees that are dead and dangerous. Nobody likes this job, so unless I do it, or pay someone to, it doesn't get done. I don't do the sawing, but I get to haul them away. Even when I pay someone to it, it's the last job anyone wants to do.

Our daughters used to love the show *Dawson's Creek*, still. Lots of television programs never show the mess that a hurricane leaves behind, but they did on this one. I was amused to see Dawson riding around his folk's place on a lawn mower with a wagon attachment. He was going around picking up all the limbs and debris that a storm can leave behind. I would tease the kids, and say as much as they liked the show, why didn't they want to emulate Dawson and clean up the woods a little. I never got any voluntary takers.

We constantly have to be on the lookout for branches or trees that might be the next ones to fall. Not just the pines, but oaks and other deciduous trees as well. We make a point to warn everybody the spots to avoid where a tree or branch could fall and kill you. In the hurricane year of 2004, it rained so much that the trees became heavy from being constantly wet. Several people were killed that year from trees falling on them. One lady was sitting under a tree in one of the state parks, when an oak branch weighing several thousand pounds, fell on her crushing her instantly.

One morning this summer, I had been several hours cleaning up branches and sticks by the chicken yard. Now I knew one of the big pine trees close by was dead and could go down at any time, but I didn't think it was going to be that day!

That afternoon I was on the porch, when I heard a loud crash come from the same direction I had been working. I jumped on the golf cart and headed that way. The tree had crashed over the fence crushing part of it and if I had been there a couple of hours later, it could have killed me. One day I showed my husband an oak with a large, dead branch on the border of the Preserve. It also looked like it would stand for a while, but then we had some gusty winds before a rain. It came crashing down over a spot where we drive the golf cart every day, down to the fish hole.

Friends and Family

Sometimes we play the game, "there are only two types of people." You've heard it. There are only two types of people, those who love the beach and those that hate the beach. One other way is to distribute people into the camp of dog people or cat people, though, of course, some like both. When we had the nursery for so many years, I was constantly surprised by how many people didn't like, or more often were frightened by dogs. Our dogs were the gentlest most agreeable beasts on the planet, but they were always barking at something.

There's a lot for them to communicate their disapproval of out where we live. Everything from squirrels to hot air balloons gets a full, "what makes you think you have the right to be here," bark/ lecture/ interrogation. The runs and dog houses were out back, fronting on the quiet old road, several hundred feet from the nursery, but they were still pretty loud. We were so used to the background music they provided, we barely noticed it. No dog ever ran outside the fences, or off leash, but considering the way some people let their dogs run loose our customers had no way of knowing this. I was sometimes treated to a fairly steady stream of women, and sometimes men ,asking me in wide eyed and obvious horror if they were in any danger. Loving dogs the way I do, I never realized that so many people feared them. This came as quite a shock.

The two most influential dogs we have known in the last few years couldn't have been more different, Bella, a regal red, fawn greyhound and Boomer an English bulldog. Boomer never lived across the hard road on our old grove property.

About a year after we moved here, my husband and daughter, who had both always wanted a Bulldog, decided in the summer of 2002, they didn't want to wait any longer. I always get to be the voice

of reason in these situations, but this time there was going to be no stopping them. They were determined.

Of course we had to kiss a few frogs before we found our handsome prince. Many of the dogs we went to see weren't even English Bulldogs, but American Bulldogs, Olde English, or even pit mixes. One day we were going to saddle up for one more try. We had talked to some folks up in Spring Hill, just north of us. When we got to their lovely home, the lady of the house had just walked outside with a small brindle male. He was charging impatiently ahead and looked happy to see three strangers. My daughter and I whipped our heads around, looked at each other and said, "Oh he is cute," as if we were expecting that he wouldn't be. He was pretty small for a bulldog and we could tell my husband was calculating he was a runt and that wasn't a recommendation. We'd made up our minds though and in this, our daughter got to be the decider. We wanted to do a little inspecting. Were the parents and other dogs on the premises healthy, friendly and well and cleanly cared for? They were indeed. The two potential obstacles was his age and the fact, they freely told us that he had been taken on approval and returned twice before. At three and a half months, he would be a little more difficult to train than if he was younger. They were willing to let us take him on approval. What's the worst that could happen? We could always return him if we couldn't manage to get along with him. We were going to make sure that didn't happen though. He was a lot of money, at least to us, $1,250, but for a bulldog it was a bargain price, due to his age and previous returns.

We took him home. He seemed perfect, with only one or two little drawbacks. He took a fair amount of time to potty train. That was ok, we didn't have jobs off the property, but it was one step forward, two steps back for several weeks. I sympathize with people who have very little time to train a new puppy. After a few months of chewing and barking and peeing in the house, I can see how it sometimes doesn't work out between a puppy and its new folks. I'm too stubborn for that and we already loved him too much. The only time we almost sent him back to his first family, was out of fear, not frustration.

Bulldogs can be prone to seizures, especially if they become overheated, over exercised, or suffer any other kind of stress. They also have an unusual flap system in their throats, that makes it hard to give them pills and easy for them to choke.

About a month after we got him, he experienced a seizure episode in our family room. He had a couple of minor ones before and they were disturbing. He came out of them quickly though, so we just kept our fingers crossed.

Our vet had given him good marks, his teeth were straight enough that he should have no toothaches or face pain. He was lean, but not skinny and every other health possibility checked out well enough. Then he would completely collapse, fall over on one side and began to tremble and flail helplessly for what seemed like forever, but was really less than a minute. We had to administer smelling salts, in the form of lemon juice and get him as cool and still as possible.

We were scared to death. My husband often accuses me of killing, or at least endangering things with kindness. I've put dog's side by side, thinking they would get along well and then they would fight. I've fed stray cats that would wander into the dog runs and get killed, well you get the picture. We didn't find out for months until Christmas, when I spent a small fortune on toys for him, that it was his toy collection causing him to have his occasional seizures. Of course some toys, Kong and other brands, are virtually indestructible, but the cheaper ones will chip off little bits of rubber or plastic. Boomer as we called him, was ingesting small bits that he tenaciously ripped off his toys. When I switched him to boiled beef bones, rope toys and the indestructible variety, our problem was pretty much over. He didn't have another seizure for three years and by the time he did, we could quickly determine the cause and administer what he needed.

When emotion was building to get a second Boomer, our son-in-law, Kevin shuddered at the prospect. Oh, he liked Boomer, everyone did, even my mother who barely tolerated dogs. She was a cat person. It's not the bulldog he fears; it's his incorrect perception that they are high maintenance. Any breed specific book, the AKC website, or others, can tell you what you need to know.

All I found that was absolutely essential in the way of special maintenance, was to wash his face about twice a week, to clean the folds in the wrinkles on his face and neck. I used a few drops of Listerine in water with a soft cloth, no big deal. It only took about five minutes a week. He could also have skin problems and eruptions, again not much of a problem. Tea Tree Spray, or some kind of moisturizing spray like avocado, helped a lot.

The main threat he faced was from the brutal heat. I'm a big believer in fresh air and sunshine, for everybody, but he could only take it in measured doses. He had a shady little yard, with a cool doghouse, called a Dogloo. But, depending on the season, he could only be outside during certain hours of the early morning, or in the late afternoon. Other than that, he was really no problem at all.

Chickens, other barnyard birds and rabbits, have highly evolved flight responses. A dog coming into their sightline usually sends them running in the other direction. For some reason we could never fathom, Boomer could walk among these flinchy beasts as if he were one of them. Even when he was a fairly high energy puppy, he never ran at them or showed any interest in them whatsoever. If they elicited any response, it was the same sort of detached disdain that he also showed for puddles. From the time he was about a year old, he could walk among the animals we knew, even some of the wild ones, as if he were one of them. The only animals he deigned to notice were puppies, some adult dogs and cats. He was a fan of the former and not so much of the latter two.

Little puppies excited him more than anything else. He seemed to be a bit weird where they were concerned. He would gently roll them onto their backs and lick everything from their privates to their necks. He had to be supervised, so he wouldn't get them too wet.

He never met a cat before our daughter Charlotte moved next door and accidently acquired one. She and her boyfriend fixed the place up really well after my mother-in –law passed away. It saved both of them from having to pay rent and with some of the savings, they had a covered porch built onto the back sliding glass doors.

That summer, on a rainy night, they heard a horrible screeching coming from beneath the house. The sound subsided, but by then they were really spooked. They got a spot light and proceeded to shakily see, what was making the noise. It came from a pretty little black female cat that had four tiny white paws. She was a teen-ager reckoning in cat time, about eight or ten months old by the looks of her. Even though she looked friendly she wouldn't come to them, because, she couldn't come to them. She tried, but her tail was caught in something. Closer inspection showed that her tail was already about 90% detached from her body and the incentive of seeing someone she thought could help her gave her renewed incentive. Within a few minutes she had pulled loose, and was headed to the twenty-four hour vet. She was fine within a few days and grew into one of the best, most agreeable cats, I have ever seen.

Boomer had always made himself at home at the house next door, so he was somewhat perturbed at having what he considered an unnecessary animal in his other house. That was just rude! When he first saw her, he didn't attack, that was not his style. Cats are curious, so of course, she came to investigate this small wrinkled blob. That's when he pounced, just harsh enough to rattle her and make her slap at him with her paw.

That "Thing" In the Woods

After that, he lifted his chin up in disdain and decided to study the ceiling. From then on when Boomer came into the house, it was time for Pacey the cat, to go outside. She would often seem to me like

she could be in more than one place at a time. She could be beside my porch and then down by the woodpile in less than two minutes. I could barely get there as fast as she could, full speed on the golf cart!

Now when I say wood pile, you're probably envisioning something completely different than what I'm talking about. This "wood pile" is the accumulation of over ten years worth of Pine limbs and trunks, Oak limbs; Orange limbs, palm fronds, weeds and other garden waste that we had to put somewhere. Over the years this "pile" has grown from six to eight feet high in some parts, and around a hundred feet long. It curves around trees in a low spot on the property between the field and the hard road.

Every month or so, weather permitting, we take the tractor and push the wood we have dumped farther into the pile. It's not as ugly as it sounds, but it is kind of a shock to think that all this is stuff we've picked up, or sawed and hauled off. Sort of an achievement, though not a fun one. It looks sort of like a twisted wall that was once alive. If you have ever read Steven King's book *the Pet Semetary* you might have some idea of what it looks like.

Now this thing has some air pockets and crannies to be sure, but it's pretty solid, so I was surprised to see Pacey vanish from the top of the pile, where she had been sunning herself, into the wood below. No doubt she was after mice or some other delicacy. I got used to seeing her down there and sometimes Boomer was with me on the golf cart while I was making my rounds. The first time he saw her on top of the pile was the first time he had deigned to notice any animal in a long time. He stared in amazement as she alighted from her lofty perch and came down to greet me. Still, Pacey was returning to her old stray cat ways and as any stray cat can tell you, that kind of life is high risk.

A few months later, Pacey vanished for a couple of days and several days after that she became very sick. She'd been poisoned, but we were almost 100% sure it had not come from anywhere on our property. Even something as quiet as a cat becomes a sorely missed companion after a couple of years. After a decent period of about six months, it was time to look into getting another pet.

They Came for a Cat Named John Wayne and Left with a Dog

Named Clint Eastwood

Our daughter and her boyfriend are good friends with a young man that works as a coordinator of volunteers at the Humane Society of Tampa Bay. Once they were ready to take in another cat, they called Ben and had him be on the lookout for a female cat that would be similar to Pacey. He called them one weekend with a very sincere recommendation for a male cat that in every other way fulfilled what they wanted. He had been given the name John Wayne

Often animals come to the shelter with no way of knowing what their name is, or even if they ever had one. These animals are given names, usually after some physical characteristic or personality trait they have. This male cat was the strong silent type, Pacey in a male form, hence his name after the strong, silent, American film legend. They liked him right away and decided to give him a whirl.

Charlotte had previously adopted Freddie, a handsome older, hound beagle mix we had for about a year and a half before he suffered a fatal stroke, so they were familiar with the paperwork requirements of adoption. Since it was a busy Saturday and there were thankfully a lot of people acquiring new family that day, Charlotte and Kevin decided to walk around and say hi to some of the dogs while they waited.

While they walked around, of course they saw cute, lovable dogs all over the kennel, but they kept coming back again and again to one. He was what has been cleverly named a Bassador, a 50-50 cross between a Basset Hound and a Labrador retriever.

He's a handsome guy, very short, but with thick legs, thick hair and big soulful eyes. His big feet are slightly pigeon toed. His color's especially cool. He's 95% black, but his face and feet have very fine, golden stripes, which sort of reminded Charlotte of Boomer's brindle stripes. This was a dilemma. Charlotte now wanted the dog and the cat. Kevin is always the voice of, "wait a minute we better give this some thought." Neither one of them wanted to be the reason a nice cat had to stay longer in the shelter, so it was with heavy hearts that they walked back to the office to receive the cat they were eagerly awaiting only a few minutes before.

It had been a busy day indeed, because there were other parties that seemed interested in adopting John Wayne, a miracle in a place where dogs are in more demand than cats. Charlotte and Kevin were now free to switch their affections without having to feel guilty. Charlotte was practically jumping with excitement. She was eager to get their new buddy to his forever home. Since he was another strong, silent type and truly had been *A Man with no Name,* they named him after another American film legend, Clint Eastwood.

We were expecting a cat, but we weren't really all that surprised. After all, there are dog people and cat people and Charlotte and Kevin are definitely the former. We liked Clint immediately. People who are apprehensive about adopting a shelter dog can take it from us, that all but one of our numerous experiences have been as close to perfect as anyone could dream of. The only negative experience we have had was about twenty years ago when the kids were in grade school.

Our Border Collie Brownie had been on duty guarding the nursery at night. The kids and I would walk him and his companion, our Schnauzer, who was named Schnauzer, down to the nursery every evening and put them in side by side dog houses, that had sturdy doors with sliding bolts and back up clips. They were there to back up the motion sensors and security cameras we had installed. One morning I went down to walk the dogs back home and Schnauzer's dog house was standing empty with the door wide open. She had to have been stolen because, we checked the locks before we left at night. Brownie wasn't talking. We were very fond of him, but we needed another dog there at night too.

We went to the Pasco County Animal Shelter. We took to a fluffy black medium sized dog called Bo. He seemed friendly and engaging. About forty-eight hours later, he got away from me and took off. After hours of fruitless searching and asking around, someone we knew called us and told us a dog matching his description was up on the corner of County Line and Cypress Creek Road chasing cows. We headed up there. We ran around the outside of the fence and then, inside the fence. He knew we were there. He would run up to where he was just out of our reach, leap up into the air and take off again. He seemed like he could keep running for hours and a black dog running around on a dark night, in a cow pasture by a busy road was either going to hurt himself , a cow, or someone in a car.

About midnight, he bolted south through the woods toward Tampa. No one could catch him and the way he was running, he may have never been caught. God only knows what kind of demons and memories he was running from.

Our other adoption relationships have been wonderful and Clint deserves to be right up there in the hall of fame. Aside from occasionally being a little nervous around our son, Clint is the calmest, sweetest guy ever. You've probably never had such a clean and polite guest in your home as Clint is in ours.

At first when they would both be at work or school, I would just go walk him a couple of times during the day. Every time I went, he was sitting quietly by the door, not lying down, his usual posture. He would look so relieved to see me that I just brought him home with me and on days they aren't home he stays here. Boomer was actually fine with him as a guest; it was when he was the host that Boomer became agitated. He thought of everything on this property as HIS property. After several weeks of us thinking that Clint was his

new best friend, once he entered Clint's house, he calmly walked in, lulled us into a false confidence and lunged across the room at Clint and tried to bite him. Well, Clint was ok with Boomer's perfectly reasonable desire to be the boss, so when Boomer came over for the day, he just went to sleep on the bed with the door closed.

Old Dog no Tricks

Everybody gets old and bulldogs sadly, get old faster than almost any other breed of dog. Originally they were big strong dogs with big strong hearts, but human intervention seldom makes anything totally better, just different. Of course there are always unintended consequences that genetic manipulation and " breed improvement" can bring.

The Bulldog's original purpose was for bear and bull baiting, which by the mid 18th century, under the influence of protestant anti-cruelty movements, began to be frowned upon. What was intended to be a kind Christian response to cruel sport which victimized bears and bulls, had the long term effect of being unkind to the bulldogs.

Throughout the centuries when they fought, they had much longer noses, designed to be able to intake and process oxygen efficiently while they held their prey in a bulldog death grip. To withstand hours of clamping down and being violently shaken by a much larger animal, they had strong healthy hearts, predisposed to efficiently process oxygen as well.

There was only one problem with these previously popular entertainers. Even though their owners and trainers protested to the contrary, they had a reputation of being vicious and unpredictable. With the decline of baiting sports, the number of bulldogs in Europe and America declined very rapidly. While they still had their ardent fans and defenders, the venerable old breed was in danger of becoming extinct.

Change, but not for the Better

There was only one way to save the bulldog, but he would never be the same again. If you see portraits of bulldogs such as *Picture of a Bulldog*, Phillip Reinagle's 1790 work, you see a lean, tall, unwrinkled, athletic dog that looks much like a modern Boxer. As we have done with every domestic animal, we began playing God with our boon companions.

By the time Great Britain passed the *Animal Cruelty Act of 1835*, some bulldogs were being bred to be shorter, wider, heavier, and decidedly more wrinkled than their ancestors had been. Their noses were also getting shorter and flatter in the front. They were once again gaining in popularity and numbers. Toward the end of the century two distinct body types had emerged, a taller, still athletic type and the shorter, squatter variety that was rapidly outdistancing them in numbers and popularity.

In 1894, the Bulldog Club of Britain sponsored a race between one of each of the Bulldog physical types. The taller, lighter type was represented by King Orry, the shorter, stockier dogs were represented by a champion named Dock Leaf. The challenge was to reach a destination twenty miles away first. King Orry easily mastered the challenge, but the bulky Dock Leaf became too ill to continue before he could reach the finish line. Despite this public relations shot in the arm for the old style Bulldog, people had already made their emotional, yet ill informed choice.

The short stocky fellows became so popular that by the turn of the twentieth century fine examples of the breed were fetching as much as $5,000. They are so beloved that they are used as the symbols for the tenacity of the British people, the United States Marine Corp, Harvard and the University of Georgia. Today, a total of thirty nine colleges and universities, in the United States alone, use them as a symbol.

Prices of bulldogs have never gone very low due to their popularity and tendency to have small litters that sometimes must be delivered by Caesarean section due to the size of some of the puppy's heads. In modern times some animal lovers have become concerned that genetic manipulation has been taken too far. A BBC documentary which was also shown on PBS, exposed ridiculously long dachshunds, whose legs cannot support their own weight, herding dogs who are too tall for the strength of their hips to bear, and, of course, bulldogs. Some of them have too many skin folds for good health, with noses too squished to process oxygen and too much body mass for their hearts to be able to support.

By the time Boomer was around seven our veterinarian had some bad news for us. He told us that our healthy looking boy would probably succumb to the number one problem facing aging Bulldogs, a heart condition. He advised us that there wasn't much we could do that we weren't already doing. We were already keeping him on the lean side, keeping him cool and aiding his breathing with a fan blowing into his crate while he slept. We also gave him constant, but limited exercise. He showed absolutely no signs of his condition, thank goodness, but by the time he was eight and a half, he began to show signs of slowing down.

Change, but not for the Better

As he grew older and slower, and we were absolutely sure he wasn't going to run away, we gave him the freedom to wander around under supervision. After he was about a year and a half old he would seldom run. By the time he was seven he was so placid and slow moving that we seldom worried he might make a run for it. Sometimes when Charlotte invited him over, I would just say, "go see Mama," open the door and let him wander over there slow and straight like a good little boy. Then he would stand on the steps quietly demanding to be let in. At first I would follow his slow lumpy little walks to the other house at what we called "Boomer speed," but he never gave me any reason not to trust him.

In June of 2011 our air conditioning broke down. Of course it was the busy season, it was going to take a couple of weeks to get fixed. Boomer had turned nine that April. I tried to compensate with cool sponge baths and showers The evening of June 26, three days before my birthday, I let Boomer out the back door and watched him head down the stairs and vanish from our lives forever.

I was sitting on the porch reading a book and lost track of time for a few minutes before I thought to go look for him. I looked over the rail to the back garden and couldn't see him so I ran down the stairs. He was lying right by the porch, beside a Roebellini palm. He looked as if he had just lain down and gone to sleep. We were devastated, still are sometimes. The wall above his crate, a wall in the living room and several picture albums, attest to the place he still holds in our hearts.

Sitting Pretty

I would never want to live anywhere else, for very long. Sure, I love to travel, but I'm always pretty happy to come home. Every winter, I'm filled with admiration and respect for everybody who lives in a cold climate. It must take an incredible amount of energy just to get dressed in the morning. The boots, scarves, hats, coats, tights, yikes. It would make me want to go back to bed before I even got up. No one has ever accused me of being lazy, even for a second, but there's no way I could cheerfully face shoveling my driveway every morning, just to go to work. Most of the time we just throw on a pair of shorts or jeans and a top, about 340 days a year. Occasionally, every five years or so, it increases by about twenty more days a year when the nights can go below freezing. Occasionally we'll have a winter with a lot of cool, cloudy days instead. We still know we have it good, and we're duly thankful. We know that people from all over the world come here, or want to come here, so we're mindful of the fact that we were lucky to be born here. I used to tell our kids that if you were born in North America, or other developed parts of the world, it was as if you'd already won the lottery. The rest was up to you.

Now, while I'm proud of the place I live, my house isn't that great. When we were blessed, and I do mean blessed, with the opportunity to sell our grove in 2000, we were very, very lucky. We could have kept our orange grove going easily enough, but there was no way we could ever make any money growing citrus again.

The only way we had been able to make a decent living was because my husband had the foresight to sell directly to the public, and to have an amazing variety of citrus. This way we could have as wide a customer base as possible. We picked and washed the fruit ourselves, except for extra Navels and Red Navels we bought from his Uncle Paul. We had Navels, Red Navels, Hamlins, Valencias, Amber Sweet, Parson Brown and Blood oranges, just to name a few, and equally abundant varieties of tangerines, tangelos, lemons and grapefruit.

Most people don't realize some of the fruit you eat you can't pick. You can pick it, but, tangerines, lemons and some grapefruit need to be clipped off the tree or you might tear a hole in the fruit, exposing it to the damage of germs and bugs. By the time I had been clipping and picking fruit for over a dozen years, my right hand and wrist were starting to hurt quite a bit, but the most important problem we faced was from the county of Pasco and the state of Florida.

Our bread and butter was our high visibility on busy, four lane, State Road 54 and the long circle drive that gave us two points of access onto the road. Between the fruit in the fall and winter, and the plants and flowers twelve months a year, we were able to take care of our three kids and even save a little sometimes. We had two reliable moneymakers, Mandevilla vines and Pummelo grapefruit.

Mandevilla come in pink, white and now, red. They grow super fast in warm weather, so we'd pay in advance to get on the waiting list for little plants that in the nursery business are called liners. We planted them in increasing sized containers, first gallons, then three gallons and then sevens. We'd sell some as gallons and threes, but our best profit came from the sevens. Aside from about 50 cents worth

of bamboo, $ 1.35 per liner, three to a pot or four if they were small and about 40 cents for the pot, all they took was a little time, water and fertilizer. They must be inspected daily for a fuzzy, orange, stinging caterpillar, but sometimes whole seasons go by without them. They grow as much as a foot a week, so all you have to do is wait a few weeks for them to be ready to sell for $20. I just paid for our annual nursery license a few weeks ago so that really brought back memories.

The only hard work about them was bringing them in every night. We displayed them along the road in front of the grove, because all that pink was very eye catching. They were just a little bit too tempting a target for the thieves among us. Occasionally, especially when we first grew them, someone would pull off the road down at the end of the grove and heave one into their car or truck and take off. There was no way to protect from that kind of occasional loss. At night we could put them inside the pole barn that served as our nursery office and was visible from my mother and father in laws house. They had dealt with people who stole from the grove for many years and while they hadn't earned it, they had a reputation as being the kind of people who could be rough on trespassers. I could have been happy doing this for the rest of my life, especially once we began making enough money to enjoy life a little.

Our other big money maker was once again, thanks to my husbands' forward thinking. It was his idea to start growing the strange, giant grapefruit he'd seen at the wholesale citrus nursery, that was owned by a Viet Names family. Like other grapefruit, they come in pink or white, but they also come flat or pointed. They can be huge, with a fine one being a foot or more across. The poetically inclined Asian people, called the pointed ones mountains and the flat ones clouds, or cloud pillows. We asked around and there seemed to be a pretty strong demand among the Asians and Europeans who were more familiar with them, many Americans had no idea what they were.

We started with about twenty trees and quickly began adding to them. Another one of my husband's good ideas was to plant the trees much, much closer together than they had ever been planted before. We had experienced a total wipeout in the late 1980's. One night, despite diesel heaters, burning tires and every other precaution we could take, every tree was so frozen that they were completely dead.

Once the dead wood was cleared away, we had a blank canvas on which to replant. Luckily we had salvaged most of the nursery stock, by laying the pots down in piles and covering them with insulated freeze cloth and keeping the sprinklers running, so the ice would stay at 32 degrees. It pretty much wiped out our ten thousand or so in savings, because we had to buy more trees.

This caused a little controversy between my husband and his mother. She wasn't opposed to planting different kinds of trees, she just didn't want to plant them closer together than they had ever been before. Traditionally citrus trees were planted fifteen, or sometimes as much as twenty feet, apart. That was the way it had always been, so that was how she thought it should be then.

Jimmy argued that if the trees were closer together, it wouldn't hurt them and you would get a decent sized crop in two to three years, instead of five to seven. His dad had his back on this one. I did my best to stay out of the line of fire. She wouldn't budge, so Buster, Jimmy's dad said we may as well do what we wanted. We were buying the trees. There wasn't really much she could do about it but fuss.

We spent what little free time we had that spring planting, weeding and setting up irrigation for the young trees. They grew well, so we had a small but healthy crop starting again in the fall.

The few grapefruit we got that fall pretty well whet the appetites of our Asian friends. As soon as the fruit started to grow big, they were literally begging us to sell them. The fruit gets big months before it gets good. There isn't much juice in these anyway, and in the summer they're hard as a rock.

Some of the lady customers would start laying siege to me by late June. They would just have to wait until September, the absolute earliest I would sell any. The great thing was, most of these advance customers didn't want them washed. They lasted longer that way and as they bought them in large quantities, they wanted them to last longer. It sure was good to not have to wash them; because it was really time- consuming since you could only do a few pieces at a time in the fruit washer.

A fruit washer consists of a small conveyor of rotating brushes with water washing over the fruit from hoses in the top. Even though we soon found that the flat, pink grape fruit were better tasting and more popular than the pointed white ones, we had no problem selling all of them every year. The price varied from about 40 cents for a small one up to about $1.25 to $1.40 for the biggest ones.

Some weeks that's about all I did in the fall, from late September until around Thanksgiving. It was fine though, it was a nice break from dealing with the public. It was pretty out there and I could play the radio, listen to music or talk shows and enjoy myself. The only down side was that the trees had to be bushy so the lower branches could help support the heavy fruit. I usually tried not to think about it, but if I crawled up under a tree with a poisonous snake under it, I could have been a goner. Sometimes it was hard to keep up with all the fruit picking and washing though, because some of our Asian wholesale customers ordered up to six hundred pieces a week. And there were several of them. There was the other fruit to pick and wash as well, they paid for a lot of Christmas presents and a few other goodies though. I would have been glad to do this for the rest of our lives.

That wasn't going to be the case. In 1996 we had another devastating freeze and even though the orange grove didn't suffer any permanent damage except for what was left of the year's crop, a power failure had caused the sprinkler system to fail and every plant in the

nursery was dead. They looked like they had been blow torched. Out with the old and in with the new. We had full time employment landscaping and getting the grove back in shape, so we closed the nursery during the spring and summer and opened back up for fruit season.

We still grew some vines and a few other flowers we could take out to sell for some extra cash. About this time my husbands' Uncle Paul had passed away and the opportunity to buy his place on the other side of the hard road came up.

Uncle Paul was a good old fellow. We helped each other out. He had a nice, little navel crop every year, and we could pay him $3.00 a bushel . He could make more money than he could have gotten if he sold them someplace else. He would bring eight or ten "bushels" which were really seven gallon nursery pots, which are about the same size. He'd stay and talk for a while about fishing, or World War II or just stuff in general. His wife had been my mother-in —laws sister and had passed away years before,, but he seemed like a pretty contented guy.

He would often tell me that when he died he hoped that we would buy his place. He figured his son would want to sell it within a few years and he figured right. His son, Junior offered it to us in 1997 and we were happy to take it, though it was of no material use to us at the time.

The late 90's were a time of turmoil for our family. Aside from the freezes, we knew, despite fighting zoning and the Department of Transportation for the past dozen years, the state was going to straighten the hairpin curve in front of the grove and while they wouldn't close the road outright, they might as well for commercial purposes. Instead of being main highway frontage, the road in front of the grove would now be on a surface road, not the main one. We'd seen this ruin other businesses in other parts of the county before.

When it rains it pours. My father-in-law was diagnosed with cancer and passed away in 1999. Even though the property wasn't going to have the value it once had, my mother-in-law decided this was the

best time to sell. The market was at a high then and there was a large shopping mall, a property of regional impact as it was called, planned for land just behind my sister-in-laws house across the highway. This was definitely a selling point.

The property was for sale for just under a year. We had one unusual incident where we met up with a real live, would be grifter. There was an older gentleman who came around showing interest in the place. We did a little investigating and found out he'd made offers on several pricey parcels and was said to be invested in several established, local businesses. Nice car, nice clothes, courtly manners, what did we have to lose? Well, not much except time. He gave us an earnest money check for $25,000 to secure his right to buy. We breathed a sigh of relief thinking our wait was over and then we began hearing strange things about the old gentleman.

One morning we were out working at the pole barn, it was fruit season and a young man came by with an urgent and worried look on his face. He owned a long established business in Land O'

Lakes. We knew the place and were curious as to what he wanted to tell us. He told us that our supposed benefactor was a distant relative of his, who while he had had a great deal of money at one time, currently didn't have a dime. He had been staying with him and running up bills on all his credit cards till he was about to tear his hair out. The old gentleman had obviously suffered some kind of break down, but while they had our sympathy, we had enough problems of our own. We tore up the contract we thought was going to make our fortune and went back to looking for our handsome prince or princess. The check of course was quite worthless.

Done

Our salvation came in the form of a local, real estate developer who was a partner in the Caliente Resort nudist community. Land O' lakes is pretty much world famous for nudist resorts. He was probably interested in the land because of its close proximity to what we hoped would be the new mall property. We sold and while he gave us a generous amount of time to vacate, we knew we had some decisions to make.

My husband's sister Barbara had challenged the state and sued when they seized her property for the road project. We explored the possibility, but since the state wasn't seizing the property, just destroy-ing its value, the lawyers we talked to didn't think it would be easy to sue the state for lost value alone. We were plenty busy, so we never pursued it further. Barbara and her husband did pretty well against the state, they bought a double wide, cleared some trees and put it down on the north end of the property, till they could find a permanent home.

It was an amazing sight when they razed Barbara and Bill's house, sheds, gazebo and everything else that had been there, within a nor-mal eight hour work day. It made you think how easy it is to demolish an entire families' life, one that had been tied to that place for over

twenty five years. Truly awe inspiring, thought provoking and a little sad.

The time had come to decide where we were going to live for the rest of our lives. Like I've said, this is the best place on earth, so we never seriously looked anyplace further than three miles from our old place. The most popular finalists were seven acres across the highway, with a little creek frontage, a grove property of ten acres that was cheaper, and the jewel in the crown, seven acres, in Lutz, on a picturesque pond with a beautiful stone house on it. That was the one we really wanted, but it was a bit over what we could spend. The owner indicated to us that they would be agreeable to lower the price by twenty thousand, but that was still too high for us. Barbara was searching the better part of three counties.

The day when we would have to vacate the property was fast approaching and while we could easily get an extension, we knew we should make a decision, quick. We showed Barbara the seven acres with the house in Lutz and she never seriously considered one of the other places again. Since there was Uncle Paul's house on the property we already owned, we decided to buy Barbara's double-wide which seemed nice and was pretty new, move it across the street to some high ground and let Grandma live in Uncle Paul's old house with our oldest daughter Alexis. She would be glad to keep her company.

I would have loved to have had the house Barbara bought, I couldn't really afford it though, especially since the place on Old Cypress Creek Road was paid for and pretty much supporting itself because of our cell phone tower.

Reuse, Recycle, I Really Mean It

I've mentioned all the wonderful plants that can be had from the side of the road, but that's not the whole story. If you truly mean to care for the environment, you have to step up every interaction you have with it. When we moved, I felt really bad that I had to throw away dumpster after dumpster of stuff. I tried to give it all away to thrift stores and what not, but things just got too far ahead of us and I ended up throwing away a lot of things that might have been of good use to someone. I vowed to never do that again, especially since we sometimes go to extreme lengths for reusing and recycling ourselves.

Some things are in front of you all the time, but, you don't automatically see their potential. Political parties around here are extremely efficient. Candidates must pay a big up front bond for their uncollected signs. If they don't pick them up, the county keeps the fee. They only have about thirty days to collect the signs, or forfeit their deposit to cover the expense of the county having to pick them up.

To help out the candidates, sometimes the local parties will help collect and dispose of them. We helped out with some of the local campaigns in 2010, so they told us we could take any unclaimed signs if we picked them up at local party headquarters. My husband got busy finding new uses for these laminated, weatherproof wonders. They come in handy for any number of things. We hook them onto animal pens to keep things from digging in, or the sun from coming in. They also come in handy to use as tire supports when you get stuck in the mud, which has happened a lot lately, or as temporary shades for young vegetable plants.

The most innovative use my husband found is one I'm still scratching my head over. We own a house, down the road, on the creek. Because of all the water, even though we did extensive roof repair six years ago. eventually the roof needed more work. There's where the signs came in handy. Our handy man used them as impromptu shingles. When I first saw it, I thought it was a clever idea, but at least I thought they'd paint them. My husband acted shocked and a little bit hurt when I suggested they paint the roof. "You mean you don't like it the way it is?" His hurt expression led me to never mention the unpainted roof again. Now, I barely notice the "political sign house," though I'm sure if you saw it for the first time it would definitely get your attention.

Carpeting is one of the leftover waste products of the construction trade to make use of. Lots of landscapers also dump out healthy sod, right on the side of the road. Sod is always handy to have around, especially for building up low spots and filling in holes and eventually

it returns to the earth. Searching the sides of the road, for road trea-
sures yields a lot of truly unexpected and useful finds. About two
months ago my husband came back from his daily visit to old highway
54 to see what was out there we could use. He came back to fetch
me because he'd found something heavy he needed help with. I was
excited to see what I thought were two roughly 4' by 6'sheets of marble, one white, one speckled gray on black marble. Unfortunately
they were veneer instead of solid, but at least they weren't so heavy.
We used them short term for a floor space in the back garden and
then when it rained so much and we were afraid the garbage truck
would get stuck, we used them and other tiles we had squirreled
away to make a path to save the truck and our grass.

Desperate times and all that, we are not above strange measures
to keep our animal's bodies and souls together. About a dozen years
ago, we had a pickup truck, so we'd drive to a bread store that would
practically give us their left over bread, cakes and pies. Good for
pigs, ducks and chickens, but sometimes there was way more than
we could use in a week.

Our creative feeding sources didn't end there. We have picked up
school cafeteria food Mondays through Fridays, and my husband has
done the occasional dumpster dive.

It comes as no surprise that stores and restaurants throw away
tons of edible food every day in America. None of the stores want
the liability of someone getting hurt on their property, so some
go to extreme measures, like combination locks, fences or com-
pactors. Then there are those, who taint or partially destroy their
throwaways, but many don't. The secret world of dumpster div-
ers is probably not exactly what you think. Most of the members
of this clandestine world, at least around here, are not the sort
of people you might think they would be. They all have cars or
trucks, often nice ones, and seem the sort of people you'd expect
to see in the store, at a restaurant, or even in church. Two people
my husband has bumped into on more than one occasion run lunch

trucks. The pre-wrapped cakes and breads must seem to them to be a perfectly safe way to save on expenses. It's always been safe for the animals though.

You want to build what ?

About five years ago there was a major brouhaha just up the road in a very pretty, well maintained community. Zoning disputes are nothing unusual, probably where you live the same kinds of things happen. To the horror of several thousand residents, the Salvation Army had bought the land across the highway and was planning on building a store/donation center there. Their prospective neighbors reacted with what I imagine would be the same sort of horror that would greet a leper colony, or perhaps a toxic waste dump.

The community called the newspapers, television stations and elected representatives to make their case that the store would draw hobos, vagrants, junkies and thieves into the area. Surely no one living in such a pristine and crime free berg would be interested in shopping in such a place. So why did the charity want to build there in the first place? The prospective neighbors were sure there certainly wouldn't be any customers. Some of the locals, noses high in the air were sure, certainly no one from their community.

Boy, were they wrong. They fought a good fight, but of course they lost. There was no pornographic or prurient intent that would have of been capable stopping a legitimate business, conducted completely within the zoning designations.

We were actually looking forward to opening day. When you say you believe in reusing and recycling, you should do it. When my kids were growing up, like lots of people with kids who wanted to fit in and wear the kinds of clothes their friends wear, we spent thousands of dollars a year on their clothes, even if we had to wear cheaper stuff ourselves. We bought retail and online, not because we didn't want to save money, we were just too busy working to comb through garage sales and thrift stores.

Even though we still worked hard, when we closed the nursery our schedules opened up a lot. That's when I discovered the fun of garage sales and thrift and consignment shops. We had always sold or given away our old clothes when they were still in good shape, now we could do the responsible thing with buying too.

There wasn't a Salvation Army out here then, but there was Goodwill and a Christian Social Services Store and I began to shop there on a regular basis. I got a lot of pretty good stuff. Mainly they were mid-level brands I might have bought retail, Victoria' Secret, Anne Taylor, Express, and occasionally more expensive, Calvin Klein, Ralph Lauren, DKNY, and a few more. Neither of these stores had the variety and quality that the new store would have.

On opening day, there were so many cars that the roomy parking lot was completely full, as were the sides of the street. People were even begging the car dealership next door for permission to park there. The attention never let up, even for a day, and low and behold the same folks that had fought the project tooth and nail, began showing up to see what all the fuss was about. The cheerful color coordinated racks and inviting displays started pulling them in too.

The first week they were open, I got a black sheath Emanuel Ungaro and several other pieces nicer than anything I would buy retail. Since the store is so crowded and some of the dealer's just load up several grocery, sized carts to resell, there aren't quite as many great deals as there were. Still I can almost always find something I love and on half off Wednesdays, you can't beat the prices with a stick.

I got a really nice, pink, Guess bag for $5.00 on half off Wednesday. It was almost identical to one I was tempted to buy at Ross for $39.99. Boy was I glad I waited. The shoes and boots are a steal too. I got a nice pair of chunk heeled, Nine West boots for $7.50. All you have to do is wipe them out with a disinfecting wipe and spray them with Lysol and you're good to go My best recent find is a rainbow striped Kate Spade bag I got for $7.50.

Don't forget garage sales. Fall and spring are garage sale season around here. There's just too much chance of getting rained out in the summer, or it being too cold in the winter. There are usually big ones in September and October and then again starting March or April. We hadn't been to one in several months when our daughter told us there were going to be about five community sales one Saturday. We decided to give it another whirl.

We went to a beautiful community in Lutz first. Now, upscale neighborhoods are either a complete hit or a complete miss. Once, I did get a set of three coffee tables that would retail for about a thousand dollars for $125. These sales seemed to be a little bit of both. Charlotte was looking for cheap Christmas gifts. One year she got someone a picture for $5.00 that was so nice, she decided to keep it for herself. Nothing much struck her except a little ceramic bust of Abraham Lincoln. She had to get that for Ben, he collects all things Lincoln. She also snagged a dog water/ feed bowl combo that could be height adjusted to a dog's size. These retail for $30 to $50 bucks and this one was like new. I headed across the street and got something I liked even better. The first thing I saw was a pair of really great Nine West gold sandals. Now this was a garage sale, but it's not unheard of for people to sometimes ask practically retail for their stuff. So, I was thrilled when the charming lady of the house told me they were $2.00! The next thing was a heavy dark red croc bag. I had been adding some fall colors to my clothes, so I asked the price. It was a Murkowski bag and she told me that she'd paid $100 for it, wholesale at TJ Maxx. I found out that they retail for $150 to $350, so when she told me it was $10, I didn't even try to bargain her down a dollar. I only had tens, and I didn't want to short her change, so I got a pretty, heavy Japanese plate that already had a hanger on it and a pink glass vase, both for my bathroom that has a Japanese garden theme. That rounded out the twenty.

We headed home after one more neighborhood because we probably weren't going to top those finds.

Moving Day

We have a long history with poultry. Some of our cherished family pictures are of our oldest daughter toddling about with two extremely warm and friendly turkeys. We would have loved to have kept them forever, but when our son and daughter were old enough to start school, they were assigned a bus stop on brutally busy State Road 54. The turkeys were accustomed to following us everywhere, so of course they would tag along to see them off to school. However, domestic turkeys can be supremely unaware of their surroundings and it was a constant struggle to keep them out of the street, while minding two small children.

For their safety, and ours, they had to find a new home, far from the madding crowd. Luckily a safe home was secured for them up around Darby, where there was plenty of room to roam without wandering into a busy street.

A dozen years ago, we were beginning our move from land my husband's family farmed for generations across Old Cypress Creek Road, to land they had sold in the 1960's and we had bought back. At the time we had nineteen lovely hens of assorted sizes and about a dozen big strong roosters and one Turken.

Of course we wanted to bring them all with us, but catching a chicken is easier said than done. You would have to have the speed of an Olympic runner and the reflexes of an Olympic target shooter to catch more than one or two chickens on any given day. There is a scene in the *Rocky* movies where the hero is challenged to chase a rooster and catch it. It is a proud day indeed when he accomplishes his task, and believe me if you've ever tried it, you respect his achievement. There is only one time to catch a chicken, and that's when they're sleepy or sleeping.

Chickens, especially roosters have long days, dawn till dusk. They will often doze for a few minutes, in the shade, during the heat of the day, but their flight response remains very active. In the middle of the night it's not unusual to hear roosters crowing to proclaim their whereabouts to the night predators lurking in the shadows. This is when they are vulnerable, docile and easy to handle. It's finding where they sleep that can be a problem.

At our other place, they had varying roosting spots. Some slept in the oak tree by the garage, and some on high shelves in the garage. We had to catch them. The property was sold and the day we needed to be gone was fast approaching. Once the all night lights and human noises were gone, predators would quickly descend on them like a pack of wolves. They would be impossible to catch without a little planning.

We took three tall grove ladders from the barn and put them at varying angles against the house, by the back door. Chickens love to hop up on things, so we began sprinkling corn and other goodies around the foot of the ladders, so they would like to hang out there. We had what we thought was a lovely secure spot set up for them in their new home. It was a former tin, equipment barn, which we had divided into two sections. One side about twenty feet by twenty, was already housing two pigs and in the other roughly same size side, we had put lumber supports in for roosts and there was a handy sliding door so we could let them out each morning and lock them up safely

at night. Since our new place was literally just across the road and our new house only three hundred yards away we could just pick them up and carry them if we had to.

We're early risers, so it was very little trouble to scoop up three or four at a time, put them in a crate and drive them across the road. This would familiarize them with their new home, in broad daylight, before they had to face the dangers of the night. Of course, as we all know, nothing ever goes as smoothly as we plan. Three of the hens and two of the roosters would cut and run at the first sight of us, once they realized something was up. It never occurs to them that you are doing something for their own good. They run screaming as if you have a meat cleaver in one hand a knife in the other.

Several days went by and we soon had to move for good. Our five errant friends had returned to their wild roosts. Time was running out if we were going to move them successfully. We were already in the process of moving some of our furniture and favorite flowers and trees.

We managed to catch the two roosters just before moving day. We would have to try to catch the hens just before nightfall. We couldn't manage to get hold of them, they were always just out of reach. Because we couldn't catch them, it would probably only be a few days before they had vanished into thin air. They didn't even leave behind the usual tell tale feathers that would have signaled what their fate was.

The Call of the Wild

One of my fondest wishes is to be able to have a dog that can be an off leash companion, as we are outdoors so much. Some people around here do let their dogs run loose, but, I don't recommend it.

In 2008, while we were still getting the paper, one Sunday about 4 AM, I went down our 300 foot rock drive to see if the paper had come. Suddenly, out of nowhere, snarling and running toward me, were two giant dogs I had seen running loose, from time to time.

There was one Rottweiler and one Mastiff. Luckily, I thought to jump up and give my best lions roar at them. This sent them scurrying back to the road so that I could run into my mother-in-law's wash house. Once I stopped shaking, I located a flashlight and a heavy old shovel, so I felt safe enough to leave and get my paper.

Just now, there's a beautiful, black Chihuahua running madly all over the neighborhood. She's so spooked by her obviously, horrible, previous experiences with humans, no one can get near her. Several families have been putting food out for her, but no one has been able to get within twenty feet from her before she takes off.

Three years ago we found a beautiful foxhound wandering by the side of the road. He was very friendly and happily jumped right on the golf cart for a dog cookie. I've always admired the breed.

This dog was obviously well cared for, his coat was healthy and his teeth were beautifully clean. We felt bad for whoever lost him, so we took his picture and put it and the particulars on Craigslist. Several days later we got a response. A lady emailed us that she thought this might be her dog, but, she didn't particularly want him back! Well this made us suspicious that he was another city boy who'd been "freed" but then why did she contact us?

We have a great problem with this. We are just far enough out of the city that people bring all kinds of animals out here and abandon them to do what? Do they think they just frolic in the meadow and graze the bounty of nature? No, they run out in traffic and get run over, they slowly starve, or they succumb to any one of a number of big predators who roam the woods.

Sometimes they catch a break, like the fox hound we called Pluto. He loved to swim in the creek and run beside the golf cart, he was well mannered and friendly and we were happy to have him.

This boy had a sense of wanderlust that could not be contained. His kennel was well made, raised off the ground and surrounded by chain link fencing. The wily fellow exploited a small place where the

chain link had a piece of loose wire. He chewed and pulled enough of the fence out then he took off. We never found him again.

A couple of months ago my daughter and I were coming home from shopping when we saw a red sports car, pulled off on the side of the road. My daughter had been robbed a few months before, and that fear never leaves you, at least for a long time.

When we drove past the car, two attractive blonde girls, who looked like they might be college students gave us a sheepish wave and drove off as quickly as they could. They had left behind two precious kittens. They were so tame that we easily picked them up and put them in a laundry basket we fetched from the wash house. We took them to Ben's house where they could stay safely until they could be taken to the Humane Society.

Almost Wild Things

Over the years we have tried to "naturalize" domestic rabbits and let them free range like the chickens, ducks and turkeys. My very favorite rabbit was the gamest ladies man I've ever seen. I called him

Dutchy, like the hero in the Civil War movie *Ride with the Devil*. He was a gray and white Dutch rabbit and I liked the movie, so the name just stuck. I will tell his strange story later, but today we have Bunny Brother and Cinnamon Sister as I call them.

When our granddaughter was three, we got to have her come for a couple of months in the spring of that year. Her dad was coming to Florida to hand his jeep over to his dad, before he was shipped to Iraq. We were very frightened, for him, our daughter and grand-daughter. We wanted to make things as fun and cheerful as possible for Madeline's visit. She loves all things animal, as most children do. We had aquariums full of fish and frogs on the picnic table and we took half a dozen rabbits from their hutches and put them in a fenced area beside the pig. You may already know, rabbits dig deep networks of tunnels called warrens, so without preparation, they would be out of that fence fast. We've learned how to deal with epic diggers over the years. Rabbits have nothing on some dogs and pigs.

First you must make sure the fence and posts are deep in the ground, a foot is generally a good depth. Then a solid barrier around the inner or outer edge is essential. Poured cement often cracks on the damp settling ground, so we generally use paving stones or bricks. Then, thick carpeting is put over the ground to discourage them looking for soft dirt to dig. It's not as expensive as it sounds. Because of the housing boom that went on for so many years, free carpet was literally lining the sides of the roads sometimes. It's one of the things people discard that can be reused a number of ways.

As the pine trees began dying out behind our house, I wanted to turn that area into a tropical garden. That's hard to do when chickens and turkeys dig up young plants and make holes everywhere under the pine needles. This makes a garden stroll rather dangerous. My solution was carpet. Lots of nurseries use carpet for weed control and even though weeds aren't a big problem out there, carpet made a no cost solution to the digging. We used it to keep the rabbits from digging up the rabbit yard too. We put several doghouses in the fence,

so the rabbits would have shelter from the owls and hawks who spy their deliciousness from above. Cinnamon Sister or Caramel Corn as Charlotte and Madeline called her, was one of the rabbits released into a new home.

The rabbits did fine in their new home the whole time of Madeline's visit. They were fine until it started to get hot. There weren't enough trees there to shade them. The dog houses were some help, but not enough. Their coats started to shed a little when it got hot. We decided rather than return them to their hutches, we would open the gate and they could stay or go as they pleased. One of the females was so timid we figured she wasn't a good candidate for freedom, so we returned her to a hutch. Their natural timidity made them slow to welcome their new found freedom, so it was a whole day before all six ventured outside the fence.

In the meantime, we had two rabbits in a portable yard that made an escape. These movable, covered fences give the rabbits a change of scene and an opportunity to graze some fresh vegetation. Dutchy and gray spotted female made their escape from one of these at about the same time.

Cinnamon Sister vanished after only two weeks, but not for the usual unfortunate reason. She had indulged her natural instinct to dig a network of tunnels under the shed, to have a safe and, to a rabbit, comfortable home for a new family of baby rabbits. Someone had been busy in the little yard. It was a happy surprise when first Mom, and several days' later, six lovely bunnies began allowing us selected glimpses of them.

Two of them were white with red spots, two were white with black spots, one was snow white and one was a deep sable brown.

It had been dry most of the summer, then in July we had a couple of rainy days and all seven rabbits in the family vanished. It hadn't been rainy enough to flush extra predators out of the woods, but something had caused our flighty friends to head underground, if they were still alive. Whatever made them vanish, fear or weather, they didn't reappear for almost two weeks. When they came up into the light, they were more confident than they had been and spent more time out where we could see them, even venturing twenty to thirty feet from the shed.

There is a curious behavior one occasionally sees in rabbits, dogs and even chickens sometimes. I'm not making this up and this is not a scientific observation, it is merely anecdotal. Occasionally baby and child animals will show a clear preference for their siblings who are of the same color. This was the case with the bunnies that were now almost three months old. The two white rabbits with red spots clearly preferred their own company, as did the white bunnies with black spots. As multiple fathers are possible in a bunny litter, and biology is everything in the Animal Kingdom, this may be an example of full sibling solidarity. This left the little white rabbit and the brown one, odd bunnies out, but they learned to get along. Luckily Mom stepped in to romp and play with them.

However they spent the day, the whole family would come together in the early evening. Sometimes some of the other freed rabbits would join them. There is literally nothing cuter than watching rabbits frolic. This is when they leap up in the air and run around in circles, clearly for fun.

The venerable Dutchman would often stop by, for he had formed a slight attraction to Mom, as well as Cinnamon Sister's sister. He had a regular visitation schedule with the ladies he was involved with. He would have breakfast with a silver rabbit, visit with another mid-morning and then travel around to three or four others throughout the day. Female rabbits, at least the domestic ones I have observed, tend to stick to a familiar territory of around one-quarter to one acre.

The males range over a much wider area, though they usually seem to stay within around a five acre space. This way they can visit

74

more than one lady, though no one has ever done it with such energy and style as Dutchy. Several of the other ladies tried to start families in the next few months, but none succeeded like the original six.

Rabbit Multi-culture

When we moved out here from Tampa in 1970, I had never seen a wild rabbit before. Granted, the city was full of squirrels, raccoons, and opossums and even an occasional flock of bats hanging from the electrical lines, but no rabbits. The 70's were a period of explosive growth for Land O' Lakes, Odessa and Wesley Chapel.

As happened to so many places just outside the big city during that period, a previously 80% rural county, almost overnight, became much more densely populated and suburban. It was a wonder it hadn't happened before. A few thousand people who wanted a little spread, out where they could have some livestock, had moved here, mainly to two to ten acre spreads. The planned suburban communities were just getting started. The two main ones were then, Quail Hollow in Wesley Chapel and Lake Padgett in Land O' Lakes. The number of big, relatively clean, skiing and fishing lakes would be a big draw to this area. Then, there had still been no mass exodus from the city.

My own family had looked at land out there for years, but never could quite bring themselves to close the deal and leave the city. The mass exodus was due to circumstances partly political, partly racial and social.

The Exodus

Property taxes were skyrocketing in Tampa. Added to this, court ordered school busing had a lot of people fearful. Some were merely annoyed that their children would have to leave the schools they had known and take a long bus ride to another one. Some people's concerns were, of course, more sinister. It didn't help that this was a period when riots had shaken the nation from one end to the other.

I do have a point here. When our house was finished on Lake Padgett in 1970, there was wildlife I had never seen before, every-where. There were eels in the lake, and wild rabbits would frolic all evening in our yard. There were really no birds I had never seen before, but there were a whole lot more of them. Quail were already becoming scarce though. I had definitely never seen wild deer before, except in North Carolina.

There were so many wild rabbits that it is truly disturbing how their numbers have dwindled in the years since. I think it's just that our neighborhood is extremely top heavy with predators. The situation is probably not helped by the fact that more people, brought more poisons. This is the land of the lawn care service, and while their chemicals are not supposed to affect most mammals, it certainly seems as if it might be a factor.

Two years ago, the fall and early winter were kind to the rabbits and they all seemed to be getting along pretty well. While they don't seriously, rabbit fighting is funny to watch. Two or more males will jump several feet in the air and fly toward one another. When they land, they chase each other around until they leap into the air again. The worst that can happen is one or more will get a handful of hair pulled out. It doesn't last long, but they try to put on a nice show for the ladies.

In the evening, it seems like every one of the rabbits would get together to discuss their evening plans. This was the best of times we had ever had with free range rabbits, but in the animal world, nothing lasts forever.

About a year and a half later, there were only three of them left, the two black spotted males of the bunny family that we called the Bunny Brothers, and Cinnamon Sister. She had outlived her sister, nieces and even some of her children. We were in hopes of maybe some wild-domestic rabbit, hanky-panky might occur, strengthening their survival instincts and tempering their bright colors.

We were out gathering up bags of leaves from some of the surrounding neighborhoods about 5 AM one morning when we saw the brothers out in the grapefruit trees near the road. There were three wild rabbits with them, I hope they were girls. As for Cinnamon Sister, she is beginning to show a little age, but she's still going strong.

Who Are Your Neighbors?

Our chickens have fifteen acres to roam with over seven thousand acres of Southwest Florida Water Management sanctuary called Cypress Creek Preserve behind our property. All that wild space can hold a huge number of predators. Our former orange grove sits across the road to the east. It's been converted to a cow pasture. Cypress Creek is to our south. Except for us, their only human neighbors reside during the day, at an electrical contracting company and church, next door, and to our north. There's a seven foot fence, but they can wander under the gap beneath it, luckily they don't often.

We sold the three and a half acre property which included the 1960's era cement block house that Uncle Paul had lived in to an electrical contractor who built a warehouse and office space and rented the house to a realtor. When the realtor moved, part of the warehouse was converted, first to a cheerleading gym, and then a church which used the house as daycare space. There's very little noise or traffic and everything's quiet at night. One space has been cleverly adapted to two uses.

Pay attention to the road.

You have to be driving like a maniac to hit a chicken. They don't dart across the road like a dog, cat or rabbit. Instead, they slowly scratch around in the vines and weeds that cover the banks along the side of the road and occasionally wander a foot or two into the street. If we see them close to the road, we coax them back, thankfully, they usually come willingly, since there's complimentary corn in the other direction. In ten years, we've had two chickens run over. Most of them head the other way, but, there's danger in that direction as well.

Depending on where you live, there can be an amazing variety of predators. Size doesn't matter, in the end. Death by chicken hawk is the same as death by coyote. Here's a short list of our bird eating friends, opossum, raccoon, coyote, fox, bobcat and feral cat. Dogs can also be a problem, but, we've had people, "drop off," more cats than dogs. Bird predators are mainly owl and hawk species, whichever are most prevalent at the time. Ospreys prefer fish to poultry. During nesting season, ospreys often deposit fish skeletons on the ground around the cell phone tower on our property. Once, one fell about two feet in front of me as I walked to the mailbox.

Snakes often raid nests for eggs. A good size chicken snake might wipe out a week's worth of one hen's eggs in less than an hour. Other local snakes include cottonmouth water moccasins and rattlesnakes, but there are also rat snakes, indigo snakes and grass snakes which are harmless to humans. Poisonous snakes are mainly dangerous to birds when they strike out against some fast scratching object that accidently invades their space. Florida's poisonous snakes can't climb and many chickens will learn to nest high off the ground. Chicken snakes can climb anything and will hang in trees like living ropes, or weave themselves through fences and gates. It can be a bit unnerving, especially if you've never seen it before. We used to have several willows at the nursery and once during a period of high water, there were three of them hanging in one tree like reptile branches swaying in the breeze.

Defender of the Nest

The oddest watchdog we've ever had has got to have been our adopted Duck. Twice, he was hero to two of our hens and the potential chicks in their nests. There were two Dogloo dog houses; side by side raised about four feet off the ground. They are roomy enough for at least two hens to sit at once, which happens from time to time. Sometimes two hens will peacefully nest in the same house, or the hens will fight until one of them gives up and goes elsewhere.

One day, we thought Duck was harassing one of the hens in the doghouse. We ran over thinking to run him off, chastise him and maybe even put him inside the fence for a few days.

He wasn't harassing a hen, but, a fat chicken snake about four feet long that had already eaten four or five eggs. Needless to say, Duck was a big hero, to us, but, not to the hen, who never did warm up to him. About two weeks later, he grew even more proactive. We found him inside another henhouse where he had picked up a slightly smaller snake and was trying to shake it to death. Where chicken snakes were concerned, there was a new sheriff in town and his name was Duck.

They Sleep In Trees

Fainting Hen Turkey

fter about three years of fruitless yearning and staring longingly at chicken hen's nests, Fainting Hen Turkey finally had some luck. She vanished for several days in the way that means a turkey hen is nesting, has joined a family of wild turkeys, or has been turned into a pile of feathers. After about five days, my husband saw her searching by the shed for leftover corn in the frantic, "I only have a ten minute break today," way, sitting hens do. Even in a Florida summer when it's unbearably hot, they don't often leave their nests until midday, so the eggs are sure to stay warm.

He waited to see where she went, and she disappeared into some thick plumbago bushes around our telephone pole. She was impossible to see, if you didn't know where to look.

After a couple of weeks of discreetly watching for them to hatch, my husband looked into the bushes and couldn't see any white through the leaves. He hoped for the best, but, feared the worst. The ground was full of broken eggs which could mean something had run her off the nest, eaten the eggs, or drug the hen off breaking the eggs in the process. The third possibility was they'd hatched out and were with their mom. He looked all around and saw her behind the house in the hydrangea bushes. At least she'd made it out alive. He hoped for better luck next time. It seemed curious that she'd been sitting still for almost four weeks and was still sitting down. When he approached her, he could see a little patch of white protruding from her side. She was sheltering ten live chicks.

Turkey chicks are much easier to catch than baby chickens, they're much slower. To protect them, for they're extremely vulnerable, we scooped up all but one of and put them in a raised coop with lights to keep them extra warm. Before evening, we decided to put the other chick up too, otherwise its' chances of survival wouldn't be good. She planted herself underneath their little pen, gazing up at them, obviously pining with loneliness. When they were old enough to live on the ground in the yard and henhouse, they moved back with mom. There, Fainting Hen could happily mother a whole flock of her own chicks and chicken peeps, to her heart's content.

Fainting Hen is not an ordinary brown or white turkey, or Florida wild turkey but, a Royal Palm. They are snow white and have beautiful black markings on the tips of their feathers. The males have impressive blue and red wattles, which are the bumpy bits of skin hanging from their heads and necks. We first saw them at the Florida State Fair a few years ago, and as soon as it was warm enough, we ordered twenty chicks. We ordered what is called a straight run, which means you get a random group of males and females because sex determination is difficult at that age and adds to the cost. After about three years, there were only two males and four females left. Several of them may have taken off and joined wild turkeys that pass through all the time. The males especially will run to try and flirt with the wild hens. Some of these wild turkey groups have been visiting for years.

The male Royal Palms are far too vain. They always seem to be fanning their feathers and turning their beards blue and red as they cock their heads to one side in what they must consider a come hither pose. They're far too self involved to be vigilant guards for the hens,

always putting on a show that the hens, for the most part, couldn't care less about.

Fainting Hen doesn't really faint, but we were the only parents she had ever known and I guess, we were her authority figures. Whenever she saw us, she would prostrate herself on the ground, or hop up on the golf cart and kneel down. That's why we called her Fainting Hen, even though Kneeling Hen is more apt.

The Shock of the New

I've heard any number of urban legends about alligators in sewers and similar tales. Around here plants, insects and animals that nature never intended to be here, arrive all the time.

There's a colony of monkeys on an island in the Homosassa River who are the descendents of "extras" brought her to be in a 1930's classic, Johnny Weissmuller *Tarzan* movie. They didn't migrate here on their own, they were brought. We run into other involuntary Florida residents all the time.

Back in the 1960's there was really only one lizard species extremely common to central Florida, the Green Anole or *Anole carolinensis*. They're often called chameleons as they can change shade based on temperature, the need for camouflage, or other factors. Despite this talent, they're not considered true chameleons. A rite of passage when I was a little girl was proving your bravery by hanging one from your ear. Touching a snake skin was another rite, but, that's another story. Their teeth weren't sharp and they're so gentle that they're very easy to pick up. That was part of their problem.

For generations they had few enemies. I've seen cats and dogs catch them and spit them out, they must taste awful. They still often lost parts of their tails in the process. This was not as horrible as it seems, because they grow back. They were so numerous they were like the wallpaper of the out of doors. Their numbers were unchallenged until the mid 1960's when everything, for them, changed completely.

This began the changing of the guard as the Brown anole, *Anole Surei*, entered the picture and decimated the little green kids, stole their territory and over time became the dominant lizard species in our little corner of the world. We just called them Cuban lizards. Tampa has always had a large Cuban population. Many of the Cuban people came here before the turn of the twentieth century to staff the cigar factories. These were one of the local economies mainstays at the time.

After the Cuban Revolution, when Fidel took over, many of the Cubans who could leave had family in the area, so they moved here. The brown anoles probably arrived when more ship traffic and trade to and from the Caribbean Islands grew during this same time period. Though they can be found throughout the Caribbean, Cuban lizard is the nick name that stuck.

You would think with the abundant natural resources, fresh water and warm air available, both the native species and the newbie's would have plenty of territory they could share. No, even though they're only a few inches long, the brown lizards came in like gangbusters and treated this opportunity like the Allies treated the Normandy Invasion. For them, in the long run, this was both a war and a colonization. These two lizards have a lot in common. Both of them can change color, they're both arboreal and both throw out fan shaped colorful throat skins when they're spoiling for a fight. There is one big difference between the two. The Brown anole is much more aggressive and invasive than his green cousin and seems to covet any territory the other possesses.

In the coming decades the Green anoles populations were so decimated that I would estimate their numbers are down by as much as 80-90%, in this particular area. This of course isn't a scientific estimate, just what I've noticed from spending a lot of time outdoors. They do have one asset around here. Elephant Ear plants which have volunteered along the road and the woods make an excellent camouflage for them. If you look closely you may see them, though around your house the other lizards have totally taken over.

The Scariest Creatures in the Forest and the Most Misunderstood

Almost every place on earth has snakes, and other places have more deadly and invasive species than we do. Still, there's something about snakes that drives even strong men to states of quivering fear.

A few years ago when we still lived across the road, a male relative dropped by and found a chicken snake on our back steps. He couldn't even poke it with a stick. My husband had to come and shoo it away for him. He is not unique in this. I've seen tough, war veterans go green at the gills when they'd see the chicken snakes hanging in the willow trees at our nursery. They don't bother me much. I had a grass snake slither over my foot when I was a little girl and it didn't do anything to me. If I can determine a snake is non-poisonous, I'm ok with it.

Once, up in the rafters of the open pole barn we used as a nursery office, we had a little red, orange and black snake who'd decided to spend some time with us. He or she, was only about fourteen inches long and minded its' own business very nicely. In most parts of the country, *Elaphe guttata* is called a corn snake, but, we call these little fellows Rat snakes. I kind of enjoyed my little friend, he never made any noise and if you didn't happen to look up and see his small curled shape on the roof brace, you'd never know he was there. He was practically above my head when I sat at our desk, but, he barely moved as it was winter time, so I often forgot he or she was there. The little visitor was probably enjoying the warmth created by the roof, as it was tin.

I made the mistake of pointing his presence out to a couple of customers I thought would be amused and untroubled by it. I was grievously mistaken.

It was citrus season and when we had a couple of customers ask for curb service because they were afraid of the little snake, we knew it was time for him to be moved. My husband got a ladder and one of those grabbers we use to pick trash off the road, put him in a corn sack and took him to the equipment shed at the back of the property. He was truly a victim of irrational prejudice.

My mother in law had the softest heart of anyone I've ever known. She grew up during the Great Depression when the few thousand citizens of Pasco County hunted, fished and grew vegetables. If they didn't they were likely to go hungry. She could never bring herself to kill a chicken or a snake. Even though she could pluck or clean any bird, animal or fish, she couldn't kill any of them. This didn't prevent her from wanting any snake on her property, dead. The harmless, rodent eating snakes were the same as a Cottonmouth to her. She fully understood their important place in the food chain and had lived with the balance of nature her whole life, yet, still clung to an irrational reaction to any creature of the reptile family. What is it about this creature that frightens so many people?

Just a few miles north of here in the lovely town of San Antonio there used to be an annual Rattlesnake Round Up. These events, which still occur in six states, give prizes for the collection of the most rattlers caught by the contestants. Sometimes they're released and sometimes they are sold or donated to medical facilities that make anti-venom serums and other medications. For three years in a row, when we had the nursery I had an occasional customer with a very unusual occupation. A pickup truck with a camper type back pulled up with four to six sturdy, brief case looking objects strapped to the side. These customers were from South Carolina and they captured poisonous snakes in the swamp and sold them for medical purposes in Tampa or Miami. On the way into town, the brief case looking containers held the snakes. Luckily they didn't by their fruit till they were on their way home, when the briefcases were empty.

San Antonio was an ideal spot for one of these events, its' practically mountainous, for Florida. The area is covered with lovely rolling hills, old orange groves and a Benedictine monastery at St. Leo, the home of the oldest Catholic university in Florida .This kind of

high, dry land is ideal for rattlesnakes. Rather than lose the revenue from the event once animal rights activists began protesting it, the organizers transformed it. It's now a Rattlesnake Festival with educational reptile shows, runs, pageants, rides and even tortoise races. Even with the economic benefit the festival brings, the average Joe still wants nothing to do with snakes.

It's not Good to be Them

When we had a business that brought us into contact with people who were here as tourists, or were moving here from somewhere else, we used to get a lot of questions about life in the semi-tropics. Where are the alligators? Answer: All over the place. Why does the county spray for mosquitoes year round? Answer: Because they can make people and animals sick. By far the questions we were asked most were questions about snakes. The most frequently asked question was how do you tell the difference between a poisonous and a non-poisonous snake?

Cottonmouth Water Moccasins and rattlesnakes aren't true snakes, they're pit vipers. It's a matter of semantics and science for when most people see one, they shout, SNAKE. When you see one of these, you'll know they're dangerous, trust me. The arrowhead shape of their head is like no ordinary snake's or even the Hognose snakes which are slightly pointed. Our only poisonous, "snake," is the Coral snake.

There's an old rhyme, "Red touch yellow, kill a fellow, red touch black venom lack," or some variation. There is a lethally unfortunate similarity between the harmless Scarlet King snake, which has wide red and yellow stripes bordered by bands of black, and the Eastern Coral snake which is deadly poisonous. The Coral snake has wide stripes of red and black, bordered with yellow. Scarlet King snakes tend to be longer, but when people see the lethal combination of red, yellow and black, they tend to kill them first and distinguish the type later, if at all. The huge volume of humans moving to central Florida in the last few decades has decimated the King snakes which were common and always harmless only a few years before.

My Most Terrifying Animal Encounter Ever

Once when I was a teenager, I was swimming with a couple of friends in a private lake in a fairly undeveloped area. We sat around in the warm lake water for more than a few minutes before we realized there was a good sized alligator about twenty feet away. That got our attention. At least for a little while we were more careful.

We had two dogs which needed houses and runs. Brownie, the Border collie wasn't much of a barker on his own, so, we borrowed our daughters Chihuahua, Teacup and built a run and doghouses for them. To make sure they stayed dry we had them built about eight inches off the ground with wood floors and we sealed them with wood trim to discourage anything from getting underneath.

The fellow that built them put a little ramp beside Teacups' house because she was so little. There were was a gate into a fenced center area which acted as a run and a left facing gate to go into Brownie's run.

One afternoon I absentmindedly went in with Teacup's dog food without scanning the ground like you're supposed to. I shut the gate behind me and noticed a Cottonmouth curled up in a circle underneath the little ramp. It was less than six feet away from the gate. In a split second that seems like it lasted forever. I was scared of turning my back to open the gate. I ran past the doghouse and climbed over that chain link fence faster than I ever thought I could, and in this case, I didn't hesitate to go fetch my husband and a gun.

Living with Chickens

If you want eggs that taste better and are healthier, or you just enjoy feeding and watching animals, chickens might be for you. It's relatively easy to have a few barnyard poultries wandering around. You need to take some precautions for their safety and if you live in

the city or the suburbs you might need to check your local zoning regulations to see what's allowed.

Free range doesn't mean just turning chickens out and watching them graze, as you might guess. If you live with neighbors and their cars, they need to be in a good wooden or other solid fence so they don't get run over and dogs can't get at them. You also want to make sure they can't tear up the neighbors' lawns and flower beds. You can have chain link, but it needs to be tall and you need a solid barricade around the lower couple of feet so snakes or small chickens can't come and go. If your neighbors keep their windows open, you might not be able to keep a rooster with your hens, especially where there are street, porch and security lights that can confuse their sleep patterns. Sometimes I wake up at two or three in the morning and go out on the porch to look at the sky. When I turn on the porch light, usually several roosters will crow "turn off the light," to me. They also make a lot of noise throughout the day. We can always hear them.

Even if you have the fence, you'll need to build coops and nest boxes, so they can be protected from raccoons, owls and other animals for which fences don't pose much of a barrier. You can usually find grown poultry by putting a want ad on Craigslist, looking at the ads, or just by asking around. You can also order chicks from a hatchery like Murray MacMurry if you want specific breeds, supplies and sound information about egg laying styles, habits and pictures of the different types.

Chicks get all the nourishment they need from the egg for about three days after hatching. When you order them you usually have to pick them up at the airport, but they may deliver to the post office, you have to check. Make sure you can pick them up right away. You have to put them under lights to keep the temperature up around 90 degrees and line the bottom of the wire with thick paper until their feet are big enough that they don't slip through. For obvious reasons, the floor should be wire, as a solid surface cannot be cleaned with chicks inside. It's just easier to change paper .

The most important thing is to gently duck their beaks into water, usually once or twice is enough? It's up to you to teach them to drink when they don't have a mama around. It's best to get a regular chicken waterer. You fill them and turn them upside down and the water refills itself. You will still need to change the water every 24 to 48 hours, or it gets stale. Baby chicks can't digest whole or cracked corn, they must have mash that's made with their nutrition needs in mind. Scratch or chick feed as it's called. It looks like cat litter.

If you are thinking about getting some chickens, bear in mind they can have their down side, especially if you're not serious about caring for them. Sometimes, after the young rooster's practice crows wake them up, or the new pets scratch up the lawn or the landscaping, careless people often find a solution by, "freeing," their former feathered friends.

We live in a strange little time warp of a place, on a little over a quarter mile road that accesses a busy six lane highway at both ends. In the late 80's, people from town, still came out to fish off the

Cypress Creek Bridge, just down our road, for Speckled Perch, Bass and catfish.

Years of drought , overfishing and other hazards of the modern world have left the creek, though still picturesque, mainly filled with gars and other, "trash fish." Oh well, the birds still come to fish and people still come to eat lunch in a quiet wooded spot that features a cow pasture one side of the road and a semi tropical swamp on the other, with a heavily wooded road between them. Some of the visitors bring animals with them thinking, that they can be freed and live a placid life in bucolic splendor.

Henley

We've adopted a few chickens and roosters from these, "drop-offs." One of the sweetest hens we've ever known, we first met when she was grazing on the side of the road a few years ago. As laying hens go, she was pretty, a medium red brown, with abundant feathers, but, she was by no means young. She must have been very frightened of being alone, for she jumped up on the golf cart and always seemed most comfortable when she was in sight of our house.

We didn't hold much hope for her because she was either too old or too heavy to roost higher than our picnic table and at first wouldn't have anything to do with the henhouse. We accommodated her by putting a little doghouse on the table. It wasn't perfect protection from raccoons or possums, but it would protect her from owls and chicken hawks.

Eventually, she felt comfortable enough with the others who were too big or too old to roost in the oak tree, to go in the chicken house. For a hen, she was always a bit of a loner. She would visit with the others, now and again throughout the day, but, would break off suddenly to go do her own thing.

Henley was an indifferent nester, but, the most loving mom. Considering the bad luck she had with chicks, it was probably fortunate that she only sat on nests about every eight or nine months.

She would hop off the nest when anywhere from one to three chicks hatched out and be the most attentive mama and violent chick protector you ever saw. Even with all that, she could never keep any chicks away from doom for more than a few days, possibly because of her age. We hated to take what might be her last chance at a happy family. It often seems like hens are emotionless once they have lost a chick, but, that is not always the case.

About nine months before she died, Henley hatched out her last chick. She didn't let it get more than a few inches away from her. We should have taken it, but, we didn't, because of her age. We were sure this was her last chance at a family. She roosted in front of our porch steps, with the chick completely hidden beneath her. We left the light on and I checked her about 5:00 AM and everything was fine.

Again at 6:30, it was still dark and she hadn't moved a muscle, so I figured she was fine. By 8:00 AM she was alone, but, stayed circling the spot where she roosted until noon. She made a pitiful sight, looking for her "lost chick." She probably knew exactly what happened, but, couldn't deal with the reality.

Even though she didn't get to raise any of what she thought were her chicks to adulthood, she left a legacy. As she was the only chicken of her type we had, there's no mistaking the hints of Henley we have seen in some of the kid that have hatched out from other hen's nests.

In chicken years she lived a long life. As I said she appeared to already be middle aged when she came here, it seemed she lived to a very old age as she lived over five more years. She had gotten a little slower over the years and as she had never wandered too far, I saw that she had varied feed since she didn't graze much.

One afternoon I went out toward the chicken house for something and I saw her lying sideways beside an old pickup truck she had taken to hanging around. There wasn't a mark on her and it was broad daylight, I think she just ran out of steam and died of old age.

The Chanel 5

A strange brood of drop offs appeared on the side of the road about four and a half years ago. There were five identical, pale reddish hens. They looked like they might be sisters and were very clannish. They were unusual. We had never seen poultry quite like them before. They appeared to be a semi domestic breed, but, their looks tended more to the wild side. They were not particularly pretty. They were somewhat thin, no matter how much they ate and their heads were narrow and long. Their feathers were a dull buff red and they were sleek instead of fluffy.

The five were all fierce nesters. They would run other hens off their nests and fiercely sit them, or their own. We eagerly awaited their first hatch offs, but, were perpetually disappointed. Those girls were extremely careless mothers and I've seen some real hen negligence over the years.

From day one, they would virtually abandon their chicks to reconnect with their non laying sisters and catch up on their grazing, food demanding and plant destroying ways. For well over a year, the only way to keep their chicks alive was to gather them up as soon as they hatched and raise them by hand.

After a few times, one of the hens unexpectedly, hatched three little "peeps," and behaved with all the dedication you could hope for. As the chicks grew, one rooster turned out to be a half Turken, the other little rooster was a Black Minorca, a breed with showy red, white and black heads and flashy arched tails. The little hen was a plain squat black of the sort I call, "crow chickens." We didn't have any Minorca hens and even if we did, they don't sit nests, so it was my guess that the biological dad was a Black Minorca rooster we got in a mixed batch of hatchlings a couple of years before.

There may have been no biological ties between any of the members of this accidental voluntary family, but for slightly more than nine months, an eon in chicken childhood time, they stayed a nuclear family. A little over nine months old, the boys started going through rooster puberty. They formed a united front against other young roosters, till they were big enough and clever enough to have a good chance at long term survival.

About this time they began to spar with each other, but, that was to be expected. With their sister they stayed an intact family for around four or five months more. They would spar, flying up into the air and mock spurring each other and then one of them would storm off for a few hours. They'd then meet back up and act as if nothing ever happened. Their mother would actually join them sometimes and then leave to sit occasionally, or for a few hours to visit with her two remaining sisters.

Oddly after a while, she came back more or less for good. The Turken meets up with them in a congenial way all the time. He can't make up his mind whether he wants full time responsibility of guarding for his own hens or be a hit and run guy. He has no problem attracting a few hens, but, as he is one of the few indifferent guards of his breed, he never achieves long term loyalty. Turken's are usually excellent guards for the most part. His adopted or biological brother was left to keep the family together and has acquired a new wife we call Little Orphan Peep.

Little Orphan Peep

I've mentioned that the five sister hens were prolific layers, but, generally indifferent mothers. Two of them, the one I just mentioned and one other, over time, became fairly efficient chick mamas. Nests don't always turn out big broods of chicks and when they do, unless they are raised by hand, the survival rate is not high.

The other red Chanel 5 sister hopped off her nest one morning to follow her one little black chick. If this happens, you must either, put the eggs under another sitting hen or into an incubator, sometimes the hatch out rate is still not very high. Several days went by nicely for the mom and chick, then one morning I went down the deck steps and around the back of the porch and there she was. Mama Red

Hen lying dead with her baby chick right beside her. The baby was practicing her scratching as if there was nothing amiss. There was only a small mark on her. A small hole had been bored in her head.

Chicken hawks, wasteful natural born killers that they are, swoop down and kill chickens or turkeys and only eat a tiny part of their head. This left the dilemma of catching the chick and putting her, in the house, where she would be relatively safe.

A chick, or peep, as I call them, seems like the fastest most wily, helpless baby animal on earth, when you're trying to catch them.

For their own safety, sudden movements bring about a fast flight response and as she never went near the chicken house or yard gates, she couldn't be shooed in. When this happens, your only recourse is to wait until almost dark when a chicken goes to roost, when they are too sleepy to react quickly. Then you can, hopefully, scoop them up and put them in a coop or chicken house until they are bigger.

No luck, not even with a little fish net. She always ended up an inch or so out of reach. You think she would have gotten tired because she was so tiny. That little peep had the fastest flight response I've ever seen. After several weeks of fruitless chasing, we sort of gave up. Every morning I was happy to see she'd survived another dangerous night.

They Have No Village

There is no village to care for unattached peeps. They must find their own food and see to their own survival. Older chickens and other hens will peck at them and chase them away from the corn, if they don't have an established parent/family group to shield them. It doesn't seem to register that these chicks are their future, unless they can see them came out of their own nest.

Due to competition for food and Orphan Peep's quite reasonable fear of venturing into unguarded fields where there's a variety of bugs and greens to eat, she stayed tiny. By then we had realized she was a hen. Even at a year and a half, she was only a little more than half the weight of the crow hen, one or the other of which looks like it might be her biological mother.

For the last several months, she has been the fourth wheel of Red Five's family, though I have never seen them mate, she is clearly one of the Black Minorca Rooster's wives, or that's what I call them. She has finally started to grow, as her family plant themselves on the porch rail every day, waiting for some sort of extra snack, she tags along with them. Their favorite snack is dry dog food, or any fruit, except guavas.

Free Mickey

Humans are very strange animals, capable of horrible cruelty or naïve sentimentality. Here between the city and the woods, we get all kinds of cast offs. We are also the beneficiaries of nuisance animals people are too kind to kill, but unwilling to share their space with.

Aside from the usual dogs, cats, and chickens, we receive exotic pets and wild animals too. Once during the height of the hedgehog craze back in the 90's, I repeatedly spotted two of the little creatures in a row of bananas by our driveway. One of our neighbors was the beneficiary of a good looking iguana that wandered up in their yard. Once there was a man wandering around the hard road. He had an expensive looking cage in the back of his truck with a perch in it. He asked us if we'd seen his falcon.

Some of the craziness has abated for it's been awhile since we've actually witnessed someone dumping out a pet. A couple of years ago my husband caught a man, someone he'd gone to school with, letting mice out of a cage into the big banks of Elephant Ears on our side of the road. These weren't little white mice, but the kind that are one person's mouse and another one's rat. Since he knew the man and was pretty sure he wasn't some crazy with a gun, he asked him what the heck he was doing. He'd caught a half dozen of the little creatures and didn't want to kill them. He just didn't feel they were the right sort for his neighborhood. Oh, really! If you don't want them, what makes you think we do?

We've also had trapped armadillos freed into our woods. Nothing can tear up a lawn like an armadillo. We gain new neighbors all the time when they tear up someone's lawn, overturn someone's garbage cans or otherwise become a nuisance to people who have moved into THEIR territory. Folks will get together and buy a box trap to catch and release neighborhood nuisances. We've also been the beneficiary of freed raccoons, which are a major source of rabies, and opossums that are also major chicken murderers and egg thieves.

The second strangest wild returnee we ever encountered was back in the 90's while we still had the orange grove and plant nursery. We have gophers, no, not the furry burrowing mammal, but Highland tortoises. We like gophers, but they can dig a mighty tunnel. They're also classified as an endangered species, so while they have most everyone's sympathy and support, they have at times stopped a land sale or property development scheme dead in its tracks. We didn't catch the gopher liberator, but knew he'd been brought to us because, he had two pink hearts, two sets of initials and the number 98 painted on his back.

Orphan Peep II

This one's on me, but, things like this can happen. We have two little portable fences that we use for chick enclosures when we are raising baby chicks. Actually they're portable, toddler play yards. We bought them for our granddaughter when she was about eighteen months old, but they're good for lots of things. We've used them for leaf and vegetable composting and seed beds too. We put a removable Plexiglas top on them, under oak trees, where it's warm, but, shady and secure enough for baby chicks to grow once they don't need the lights, until they're ready for the yard.

We had two enclosures with about eight peeps in one and ten in the other. We prepared roosts and feeders inside an enclosed covered part of the chicken yard and got a cat crate to catch each set of chicks so we could transfer them to the yard with the bigger birds.

Everything went well with all but one. When you open something and make a sudden movement, a chick's instincts tell it to fly upward. Instead of opening the front door of the crate, I accidently opened the top. Low and behold, one little black chick, whose sex was yet to be determined, flew out and after two weeks, she displayed all the escape speed of her predecessor. She's much more bold

and adventurous though. She covers a wider territory in her travels, always careful to stay in close vicinity of a guarded group and refuses to be run away from feed. She seemed to miss her old enclosure as she spent a fair portion of every day sitting with the two baby ducks who became its new occupants.

The Ages of Birds

If you've ever taken a Sociology or Lifespan Development course you read about the, "stages of man," or "the ages of man." Chickens, turkeys and ducks, if they're lucky, go through similar life changes. In a reasonably safe place with adequate food, there will be communities with babies, children, adolescents, adults and the elderly, just like with humans.

In commercial egg and poultry farming, lives are finished at a surprisingly young age. Egg laying hens are thought to lay most productively between six months and one year old. Once their egg production falls, they are usually used for soups and broths. Likewise with those produced for meat. No one wants to eat a tough old bird. When left to live out their life cycle naturally, they can live out all the stages of life, though theirs are still much shorter than ours. They live on average only six years. Eight is like a hundred plus to them, even under the best of circumstances.

The human life cycle is often depicted from crawling to toddling, then walking upright and then stooping low with old age. The physical differences between a young and vigorous chicken, turkey or duck and an old one are not as apparent to the naked eye as they are with humans. It's their movements and behaviors that will give their age away.

A baby chick is even more helpless than a human baby, in most cases. Human babies are sometimes neglected or abandoned, but, baby chicks are at the mercy of nature, their physical frailties and sometimes, as with humans negligent parenting. They also have to contend with a host of predators.

Even hens that jump right off the nest to care for their hatchlings in a fierce protective way often abandon them as soon as night approaches. They jump up into the trees or eaves of the shed or chicken house, leaving the little ones to fend for themselves.

If the chicks survive the night, "mom," will usually be back on duty in the morning. The odds of a chick surviving the night alone, or in the company of other hatchlings isn't good. The first thing they do when they get frightened of the dark and of being left alone by, "mom," is to cheep loudly, allowing any predator in the vicinity know exactly where they are.

That's why it's best to catch them and put them up for several months until they're old enough to have some speed, strength and judgment.

The wild fowl chickens they descend from usually sleep in trees. They're much smaller than modern domestic breeds, which gives them mobility they use to their advantage in the wild.

Over the years, we've realized the big modern domestic breeds were helpless if they were allowed to roam free. They couldn't run very fast, very far or even fly into a tree to escape from predators. They simply couldn't do these things as fast as they should do. Their enormous size and weight caused us to slowly realize we needed to introduce smaller, quicker footed breeds into the flock.

We found that the more our original chickens mixed, their next generations tended to have the more desirable characteristics of domestic chickens with more of the survival instincts of their wild ancestors. The most desirable characteristics of both were good. The docile, non aggressive characteristics of domestic breeds help to keep the peace, but it's good for them to be tempered with the better survival skills of their wilder brethren.

Wild fowl have good and desirable characteristics, chiefly fast flight from danger. They just don't lay gigantic eggs the way some domestic breeds do. For survival these traits should be combined with an instinctive ability to find cover. They have other qualities that

help their survival, chiefly the ability to forage effectively and nest communally. Domestic hens will sometimes nest communally too. It may be a vestige of their wild origins.

Wily chicks will try their best to roost as high as they can hop and as they get older they go a little bit higher all the time. A hen or rooster in the prime of life roosts as high in the trees as it can fly or climb. Status also determines placing, but not as much as physical stamina.

After several years of having the choice of going into the chicken house to roost and have us shut the door till morning, or roosting in the trees, the majority of chickens who are small and agile enough and most turkeys chose the trees. The exceptions being the elderly domestics who were too large and slow to make it very high off the ground and the youngsters who couldn't roost very high either. Duck had the same mobility problems, but, was too independent to roost with the others, except for a cold rainy month one winter when he did give the henhouse a try.

The more in their prime of life they are the higher they climb. As they grow older, the ascent into the high branches becomes more difficult. Chickens are resourceful and oaks have branches that are springy and bendable towards their ends. Two of the longest lowest branches on the preferred roosting oak practically lie on the ground. This is from the weight of so many fat hens and clumsy turkeys using them as a stepping stone to safe places higher in the tree.

In extreme old age, sometimes they will stubbornly cling to their independence, much like so many human old folks and make it a few feet up the branch and then give up and spend the night in the spot where they can go no farther. Some grow to such an old age, like Henley, that they can't maneuver bouncy branches at all and must either allow us to shoo them into the chicken house or become easy pickings for the night hunters. Like humans they resist any feeling of helplessness and dependence and will often attempt to sleep on the ground in constant danger rather than admit they're old and need help.

A Duck for All Seasons

If you've spent any time around water, a river, lake, ocean or whatever, you've probably seen that all sorts of waterfowl can get injured and have their hunting and grazing abilities impaired. Often they can live pretty good lives, if they don't have too much competition, or they can get a little help from their friends.

We once knew a sweet old couple on Pine Island, the one off Hernando County, not the one in the Florida Keys, which took in a baby pelican who'd been injured in a tropical storm. He grew into an otherwise, healthy adult pelican, but since he could only glide a few feet, he couldn't hunt the way a pelican should. He loved to splash and fish along the shore, but, that couldn't provide enough sustenance for a bird his size, so he hung around these folks because they fed him. Their covered deck was his preferred roost.

Duck was also an orphan of the storm. In 2004, we had four back to back hurricanes, Charley, Ivan, Frances and Jeanne. Even here, almost twenty miles from the coast, Cypress Creek rose so high that fields and woods were flooded to a height not seen in more than twenty years. Our little fish hole which is several hundred feet away from the creek's natural banks, was mingled into it as the creek flooded so far that it washed over the fish hole. This allowed all of the stocked catfish and tilapia a means of escape to the creek.

Duck was not a barnyard breed. He was a wild creek Muscovy duck. The lady who took care of him didn't remember which storm had damaged his wings. They made it impossible for him to fly or run with much speed. His wings looked like they were flipped upwards in a permanent pageboy flip hairdo. In mid 2007, the lady who took care of him was going to move away and we went to look at some furniture she was selling.

When we saw Duck we asked how he got his unusual feather do and she told us about his problems. She couldn't take him with her, so, we agreed to take him with us. Immediately, Duck became about the most entertaining guy around our place.

We worried about his safety, because he couldn't roost in the trees like he should and he could be feisty if you tried to get him into a yard or house. He slept out in the middle of the grass between the shed and the flower bed around the electrical pole, at first. This made him a "sitting duck." That must be where the expression comes from. Night after night, week after week, he made it. Now, I know for a fact owls use the phone lines to survey the ground only a few feet above where he slept. I've seen them. Deer come galloping through, at all times of the night. I know because they destroy rose bushes and other deer delicacies that aren't behind electrical fences. Considering the numbers of turkeys, chickens and rabbits we've lost in the general vicinity, he was one lucky duck.

As dangers arose he would vary his sleeping place. In early winter of 2009, he would make the long trek down to the fish hole and float toward the center of it all night long. I thought this looked especially dangerous, but, he never got caught. When we would sit out in the early evenings, he would stop by our chairs before he went to the hole. It was only about two hundred feet away, but, it took him a really long time to get there.

As the weather grew warmer, he moved again. Sometimes, he would stay in the chicken house, but never for very many days in a row. He walked with a small limp and uneven gait, but, some things would get him moving at an unbelievable pace.

He was good natured with almost every creature. Boomer and he could stand or sit beside side by side, as if they were friends, he'd never ruffle a feather.

None of the other poultry were the least bit concerned by him either, as he was the least likely dog to cause a chicken any harm that ever lived. I'll never forget the time I saw Boomer and Duck sitting, side by side as if they were enjoying the sunset together. By the time I could run for my camera, Duck had commenced his long walk to the fish hole and I never got a chance at the same scene again.

Duck would peaceably consort with most creatures, chicken hens, turkey hens, chicks, some roosters and a docile dog like Boomer or Clint. He would even join the mixed group that ran to the shed door whenever we went that way demanding a scoop of corn. That often brings a mixed bunch of birds, rabbits and squirrels in a group that gets along pretty well with each other. Occasionally Duck would take an instant and violent dislike to another male or males and then, the change in him was amazing.

Duck and the Rooster

We have one exceptional large, fine rooster, bigger and stronger than any of the others we had for over five years. He's a Doppelganger for one we had ten years ago when we first moved here. He looks like a Barred Rock, an American breed of exceptional beauty. I call him Mr. Orpington, why I'm not sure, as Orpington's are a whole other breed.

He has silvery white feathers edged with greenish- black tips around the edges and red combs, to set off the black and white. We acquired him in a mixed batch of hatchlings.

This type of rooster is beautiful to look at, but, I like as much peace and as little fighting and this boy liked to fight.

Because of his size and strength, he could wreak havoc. He was so fractious we had to put him in the high fenced area where we kept our remaining goat, White Ears. We also placed two hens with him, to keep him company. The 60 x 80 foot area in front of the two little goat houses was mowed, but, behind it, there were tall dog fennels and ferns. When one of his hens went missing and the other hen was sitting, the rooster became bored, hopped the double chain link security fence and came hunting trouble.

As far as he knew, there was only one male who wouldn't turn tail and run from his overpowering strength and speed. That would be Turken Man II, who most likely was the father of the half Turken rooster I spoke of earlier. Most black Turkens are indistinguishable from one another. They weigh around a fourth as much as a Barred Rock, but have similar height and greater speed. This guy had one great signature move.

The Turken would fly up in the air, as if to spur, and spin forty five degrees or so around. Eventually this can back his enemy against a wall or other barrier and then Turken wins the contest. Once fully grown and established, he almost never fought, because he was seldom challenged. He still knew how.

I didn't see Mr. Orpington get out, but when I saw him I knew there would be trouble and since I was the only one home, I would just have to see what happened.

Sure enough, Turken Man was hanging around in the palm trees behind the house, where it's cool and he responded right away to the challenge crow from Mr. Orpington. Rather than run out into the open, he hopped up on the deck rail and sent the challenge right back. Mr. Orpington figured he had nothing to be afraid of from such a slightly built guy who'd obviously been beat so badly his neck feathers were missing. He ran right into his rivals turf in the palm trees, which worked out for one of them.

They flew up at each other. Mr. Orpington's gorgeous neck feathers were in full ruffle. Then he got a big surprise. He could jump high and strike out with his feet impressively, but with each move Mr. Orpington was a little closer to the wall. Humiliation broke up this fight before I could even turn on the hose.

Here they came running full speed through the yard. Mr. Orpington was running with Turken Man in hot pursuit. He stayed in his fence for the next couple of months suffering the indignity of some of the young fellows coming all the way across the yard to crow challenges they should hope he would never take up.

Mr. Orpington's remaining hen was one who will sit on eggs almost nonstop. This is hard on a handsome, virile rooster. He had plenty of room to wander, plenty to eat and the goat for company, but, something was missing.

His hen was absent so much of the time, it was often hard to know if she was dead or alive. Three or four times, little chicks would hatch out, but whatever lived in the dog fennels made short work of them, as we found out, she was the kind who just let them wander off.

Soon, Mr. Orpington became bored with this situation and decided to take another field trip to the yard. This time, something was different. He didn't make it much past the shed before Duck, who'd been beside the porch a little more than fifty feet away, came running as fast as his limpy duck feet could go. He didn't just want to fight the rooster, he wanted to humiliate him.

Orpy had never run from a challenge before, but, he had never been challenged by a duck before and this one outweighed him and was out for blood. Duck proceeded to chase him around the wide expanse of grass we use for a driveway and even though this rooster could fly, he must have been scared flightless. Duck was drawing the big audience he seemed to crave. They were coming out of the pasture and from around the chicken house and under the porch. I stood in awe as Duck began to gain on his enemy. I took a second to shake my head at the odd sight, but I needed to break this up.

As the rooster began to tire, I needed to get the hose to make sure no actual blood was spilled. By the time I got back with it, Duck was closing in and had pulled out a few of his tail feathers with extreme prejudice. Orpy broke away again, but he was getting slower. Curiously, Duck loves water, but, this is still the best way to break up a fight. The pressure was just enough to separate them long enough for Orpington to beat a hasty and humiliating retreat back to his goat pasture. We got him a part Aracuana hen,

which seemed to please him and he was about to begin one of the weirdest relationships I've ever seen, but, to this day, he never leapt that fence again until he noticed Pretty White Hen roosting in the tree right beside his fence. He will leap the fence and hang out with her for a little while, but he never stays for more than an hour or two.

Forced Cannibalism?

I have to vent a little. I enjoyed *the Social Network*, it was a great movie. The part that had me shaking my head is where Zuckerberg's partner has gotten in trouble because his fraternity makes him keep a chicken for a week. When he feeds it some chicken, he is brought up on charges of animal cruelty. The two guys are perplexed at him being charged with, "forced cannibalism." They should be, because clearly these chicken protectors have never actually met any real chickens. Chickens are omnivorous, which means they like to eat anything. In their case that really means everything.

They will chew up your favorite plants and flowers and eat bugs. Some of the little miscreants even eat their own eggs. They will even peck at their own dead. They do not prefer chicken to other meat, but, I guarantee you that if you throw part of a cooked chicken anywhere there are chickens, it'll get eaten real quick. The same goes for any cooked meat they can tear.

I really like being around chickens, but, in the many years I've known them, I've seen some of the same deviant behaviors we see in humans. I've seen murder, assault, sexual assault and nearly every other kind of behavior we dislike in big, dangerous humans. Just because chickens are small and have pretty feathers doesn't mean they're cartoon characters. They're real live animals and not everything they do is sweet or pretty.

My point is that ignorant hysterical reactions do nothing to help vulnerable animals and demean the real work of people who try to stop animal abuse and alleviate real suffering. It does nothing to help animals by complaining about a chicken eating something it would be happy to eat any time.

Junior Peeps and Mini Peeps

I've already mentioned that not every chick that gets hatched has an attentive parent to care for it. We had two little sets of non biological siblings hatch out close to the same time one summer.

The first set hatched about five weeks prior to the other, a long time in chicken lifespan. There were three yellow and three black chicks. At that point it's difficult to tell exactly what they will look like, especially somewhere their potential parents can mix freely. The older six, or, "junior peeps," may or may not have a biological relation to one another. As they grew, it looked as if several of them might. It turned out there was one white rooster and two white hens, and two black roosters and one black hen.

They were a good looking group. The white rooster was of a Delaware type, tall, medium heavy, but with unusual buff markings

in his head and tail feathers that are suspiciously the same color as the five sisters. The little white hens showed in their size and shape that they definitely had bantam blood. It looked likely that their mom or mom's were plain white hens and the dad or dads were the twins, Mr. Grey or one of the other bantams. They were a little more than half the size of laying hens. At first, the girls were identical and almost impossible to tell apart like twins, but, after awhile one was slightly shorter and wider. The other grew a fine band of contrast color feathers, mainly buff and black, at the base of her neck.

One of the black roosters was a black rose comb, a good looking small breed and the other looked to be a black rosecomb, small black hen combo. The hen was, due to her size, part bantam, but, because of her black color with a silver tipped ruffle around her neck it was hard to determine whose daughter she was.

Though turned out from adult supervision while they were pretty young, they maintained their close knit relationship while in the yard and when they were old enough to wander free. Instinct took over for them, most of the time. They were always together for the next seven or eight months.

The roosters developed rooster skills, crowing and guarding the group. A rooster who is a good group guard will generally never lack hens. An excellent rooster will also herd his flock away from dangerous spots near the woods, the street, the fish hole and the creek to name just a few places where danger might lurk. I've never seen a well guarded group go into the dense forest of the preserve, though sometimes they will skirt pretty close.

Unfortunately, young Mr. Rose comb had not yet gotten the memo about the street. He believed the grass was greener and the bugs tastier along the weed banks across the road.

For about a month, we had to use the golf cart, or a palm frond to shoo the junior peeps away from the road. They had started out so efficiently, but, the leader Minorca would lead the whole group to the edge of the road and beyond. Every day, we herded them back from danger.

After about two weeks of this, one morning when we took some mail to the mailbox, there the little would be leader was, dead. He was in the road a little south of the fire hydrant. It was a darn shame for the little group was now five. It takes real carelessness to run over a chicken. They're never out at night and generally move slowly enough across a road for driver's to dodge. We live on a lightly traveled black top road. It was built so long ago that modern sized cars must pull slightly to the side to let other cars pass. In country where deer and other animals can dart out unexpectedly, most of us remember to drive accordingly. The only good thing that came out of this was that the rest of the group never ventured as far as the road again, but, the road isn't the biggest danger to free range chickens.

Mini Peeps

The mini peeps were one of the strangest cases I've ever seen of creatures who weigh less than a couple of ounces having the tenacity of bulls. Essentially two small nests hatched out at the same time. Two black chicks jumped out of their nest box while their mom still had a number of eggs unhatched, so she let them go. At the same time, another hen had hatched one white chick that she seemed very devoted to.

The two lonely chicks adopted them as soon as they spotted them. This wasn't easy as unattached chicks are usually persona non grata. It doesn't pay to be shy or accept rejection, though, for sometimes they can persevere. As the hen kept her chick close and was teaching her the fine art of scratching and selecting the best things available, the two unattached peeps came up to her and stuck to her like glue. She knew they were not from her nest, so she would peck at them and run them off a few feet, but, they were stubborn. Back

they came, time after time, hour after hour, day after day. She would peck, occasionally out of frustration at being stuck with chicks from another hen's nest and sometimes perhaps because she felt she was protecting her chicks' food supply.

They never gave up. I have no absolute proof, only what appeared to happen. After several days, her little white chick appeared to take their side. When she would peck at them and they retreated, she would retreat with them. Mama did not like this. Once her precious peep had changed sides, she had no choice but to accept the interlopers or face unpleasantness with her own dearly beloved baby.

She acquiesced to the three pronged assault, at first, grudgingly. She would sleep with her own chick under her ample breast, leaving the others on the outer edges of her wings. While they scratched, she would keep closer to her own chick, but, slowly, she came around. After two weeks she had been worn down. By then, if you didn't know the other chicks weren't her hatchlings there was no way to tell they weren't a natural family. Her behavior to the black chicks was identically attentive as it was to the white chick which had hatched from her own nest.

Success, but, in the chicken world, nothing lasts forever. After four or five months of family unity, it was time for Mama to sit again. She had given the peeps a good start. They were good sized and had received all the lectures she had on survival, as well as her tips on where to find the best eats. By this time, the parentage of the chicks could be guessed at, if not assured. The black chicks were a hen and rooster, he was a half Turken. He could only be half , for as I explained all our Turken hens had been wiped out several years before. His biological mother could have been anyone, though a domestic black egg layer seemed the logical choice. The little hen appeared to have some small breed bantam in her or maybe just small crow chicken. The white hen was pleasant looking but, not particularly distinctive. They might have made it on their own, but, by this time they had become friendly with the five remaining junior peeps. They joined forces and until another tragedy struck their little community they were close.

Loners

We usually think of chickens and turkeys as preferring to live in flocks or groups. There are infinite combinations, families, comrades and loners within any poultry community. Just as some people spend substantial time alone, because they enjoy it, they're shy, or they have poor social skills, the same phenomenon occurs with animals. Among chickens, most loners are roosters, some just like to be alone and some are too despised to attract hens or comrades.

Some rooster's, don't want the responsibility of guarding hens and being responsible for someone else's safety. It's exhausting always scanning the horizon and the sky. Sometimes, they have voluntarily relinquished their responsibilities, as if it were a retirement from a job and sometimes they are just tough and quick and can mate with lots of hens without having to be responsible for their safety. They might be the lounge lizards of the poultry world, but, sometimes this gives them an opportunity to breed with a larger pool of females, so, you could argue a biological motivation.

The two identical twin bantam roosters I call the golden boys are congenial occasional companions. They're like brothers who get together to have a beer and watch a game a couple of times a week. Other than these friendly meetings which occur several times a day, one of the brothers is a loner. He circulates near the edge of small flocks when he wants to raid the hens, but, often stays completely alone. In my experience, voluntary loners are more common among the bantams than the bigger breeds.

Sometimes, being a loner is not voluntary. A few years ago when our poultry population had been depleted through old age, hurricanes and predators, we bought several batches of chicks and roosters to replace the layers we'd lost. We bought some Aracuana breed hens and roosters, mainly for their pretty pale blue eggs.

They're unusual looking, they have no rump and since they have long necks and tufts of feathers popping out in strange places they're kind of odd looking. For whatever reason, no other chickens would voluntarily associate with the twenty or so Aracunas, no one. Very docile hens that never ran from the mating attempts of other roosters would run screaming from them. The hens, while other breed roosters would breed them, were seldom fully welcomed into established flocks. So, you might think they would establish their own flocks. That's not possible as the Aracuna hens didn't want anything to do with the roosters either.

They were prolific layers though. Soon there were half and quarter breed chicks who were more easily accepted. The males were still disliked, but, not despised. There are only a handful of the original hens left and none of the roosters, though one persistently beat the odds until this spring. He had his own way of getting back at the other roosters every evening.

The Ambush Artist

I've mentioned the way an efficient rooster guards a group of hens. A long day of surveillance gets the boys hungry by the end of the day. We put corn out along the sandy drive behind our house and once the hens begin taking their places in the trees, or houses, the roosters are free to relax and eat all they want. For three years the Aracuana rooster had hung around the trees chasing the hens on their way to bed. Usually, he would get run off some thirty feet or so until he could sneak his way back into striking distance. He'd been treated pretty badly by the others when he was growing up and the best guard roosters still prevented his way into the strongest, most protected branches in the trees. Over time, he devised a revenge strategy.

As he aged, Aracuana Man became super fast. He would appear out of nowhere, popping out from under a bush or vehicle, or leaping from trees and roofs. This helped him to level the playing field.

His raids on hens became impossible to fend off and he made his escapes so quickly that it became difficult, and then impossible, for the roosters to extract revenge. He also began to extract revenge on the roosters who'd made his life a living hell.

As the guard roosters would filter back to the trees from their late supper, he would pounce, literally. He would leap out from behind something or from the top of something, startle and pounce on them as they made their ascent into the trees. Then, he'd be gone like a flash. His tormentors, knocked to the ground by his hit and run raids would jump up, shake off their feathers and frequently get knocked down again. When he was in a particularly energetic mood, he'd keep running at them till almost dark. As he was large and unpopular, he was going to be the last into the tree anyway, so this was a nice opportunity for him to give back a little of what he had received. Aracuana Man vanished this past March, but lives on in his children and grandchildren.

Over the years we have had an unusual phenomenon of a mid-sized rooster, who is on the light side who is the toughest guy in town. Right now we have a really good looking rooster of this sort. He is only about twelve inches tall and he has a slight build. He has a beautiful black tail with long, slim arcing feathers. He is a golden red with, green and black accents. Every rooster, even the biggest, strongest ones, acts like they're afraid of him. The second most feared seems to be a relative of the Aracuana hen that is in the goat pen with Mr. Orpington. They have identical gold on black with a slight bit of green coloring. However, he shows no Aracuana in his shape, he is identically shaped to the other tough guy. Nobody messes with him either.

Temporary Loners

Sometimes roosters grow up in a companionable group, like the Junior Peeps. Sometimes they lose their mom, to a new nest or through tragedy and they must fend for themselves. We have two of these now. One is a good looking white rooster with a few, buff edged feathers around his neck, and the other is a beautiful combination of red, green and green black feathers. He most resembles a Leghorn, but, free birds make unusual combinations, so you can see small bits of other breeds in him as well. Both boys have been involuntary loners since their mama's cut them loose before they were grown, at around four or five months old. We are in a rebreeding year, so we have hens setting and hen chicks growing, but, only a couple of dozen breeding age hens, none of whom are unattached.

Some breeds love to fight. Most chicken fighting is more show than lethal force. When there is plenty to eat, plenty of hens to mate with and few predators around, the stress level lowers and even the most fractious roosters can become more peaceable over time. In good times of plenty, the biggest threat to peaceful relations is the unattached sexually frustrated young male. You might notice the similarity to human society, where the same conditions of youth, stress and alienation drive some to vandalism or violence.

Two characteristics of poultry societies put a natural check on these boys running amok. Even though they are too young to attract the attention of the mature hens, there will usually be another batch of girls along soon. When this year's hen chicks are old enough to turn out of the fence, these boys will seem like the big men on campus to some of them. It's amusing to watch some of the roosters and gobblers march up and down either side of the fence checking out future mates and potential rivals.

Some of the roosters have a creepy way of checking out the chicks when they are taken from the heated coops they live in when they are babies, and put in the portable play yards for several weeks. Sometimes they circle them like predators.

I'd like to think it was simple curiosity, or admiration for chick cuteness, but, having seen some of these guys try to chase down very young prepubescent chicks for their own wicked purposes, I suspect differently. Before you are too horrified, chicks can be very fast, super maneuverable and can fit themselves under very low things for protection. As roosters' have little patience, their wicked will is invariably thwarted. While I have seen stray chicks get chased pretty frequently, I have very rarely seen one caught, by a rooster.

The second factor which keeps the young males under control is the censure of poultry society and sometimes, the intervention of human authority. When the young fellows get too fractious, retribution can be fast and furious. While no hen or rooster will take responsibility for the odd orphan, something as destabilizing as violent rogue males faces a solid wall of chicken society disapproval. I cannot explain how they do it, but it seems that rogue males who threaten stable groups are turned on by the others, with the threat that society's censure will be permanent unless they straighten up. They almost always do.

The red rooster and the white rooster have different coping strategies to deal with their teenage angst. I've mentioned the

nuclear family of the crow chicken, orphan peep, red hen and Spanish rooster, the red rooster is their permanent shadow. That's why I call him Shadow. Wherever they are, he is also. It is not hard to see him get run off by the Spanish several times a day. Sometime he is just chased, but, occasionally he is also back spurred as well. This will change because the Spanish is smaller and lighter and the red rooster is gaining speed and strength pretty quickly. It's not inconceivable that by next spring if he has a few hens of his own, they might form an alliance. Stranger things have happened in the chicken world. It's even possible that they are half brothers or have some other biological connection, because for a long while he never shadowed any of the other groups. I hope it happens, but, regardless of the biology of the situation, I believe he is going to be a successful rooster.

The young white rooster with the buff markings presents more of a problem. He doesn't shadow any particular group, instead, he waits around the porch, out in the grazing field or in the bushes and waits to ambush whatever hens come by. He has only recently had any success, so it remains to be seen whether alleviation of sexual frustration might have a positive effect on his general behavior. He can be aggressive, even with us.

When my husband is driving the golf cart he has a bad habit of dragging his foot off the side. This fellow will sometimes jump and try to spur his leg. He hasn't done it to me, but, I've seen him do it. Every day he doesn't, is a victory, because if he turns mean something will have to be done. No, not what you think, he's in no danger of being turned a dumpling dish, but maybe fenced for a time. We shall have to see.

The Dutchman

We've had rabbits off and on since our children, who are in their twenties and thirties now, were in grade school. To me, some of the prettiest, most agreeable rabbits are of the Dutch variety. These are smallish rabbits with black or gray heads and bodies with a white section separating the two.

When our granddaughter came for a visit, we wanted her to have a full animal experience. Madeline loves animals and the outside, like most little kids do. We have rabbit hutches which are safe and cool for the rabbits, but, not so safe for us sometimes. They're in a pine grove and this particular variety of pines, which were planted in the 1980's, are occasionally struck by pine borers, so it's not real safe to walk there sometimes. When they are afflicted with a mild infestation they can fight it off, or they can succumb and slowly die. The rabbits are safe, protected by a wood and metal roof, but, we don't walk out from under the roof without careful consideration. I've mentioned we put some little houses and food and water bowls in a 6 x 12 foot chain link fence and put about six rabbits in there, so we could walk out and see them. Even though the area was long ago carpeted with remnants and we put fresh pine needles on the ground, some of the rabbits' coats began to look pretty scruffy once the summer heat set in. Since one of them acted like she would prefer to be back in her hutch, we switched her, with two more who acted as if they would enjoy some elbow room. When we came back from taking Madeline home, we reckoned to free the seven rabbits in the fence. Color and breed wise, they were an assortment. A big white female with red spots, a silver fox female, a brown sable female, a black and white spotted male and a black and white Dutch we didn't know the sex of.

They were soon joined by another gray and white Dutch male and a spotted female who were in a movable grazing fence. These give them a chance to enjoy some fresh grass and fresh air for a few days. Normally, this works pretty well, but the little Dutch was a real fast digger and out they went. Rabbits are very hard to catch, so they joined the then growing free rabbit population.

We don't know why, but the black Dutch male and one of the other males vanished after only a few weeks. But, to the ladies, it was as if they'd never been there at all. All six of them were being romanced by the playboy rabbit of the western world, the Dutchman, or Dutchy.

Male rabbits usually earn their well deserved reputation as hit and run romancers, but, not this guy. A lot of human men could learn something from the attention he pays to the ladies. The silver rabbit was his number one lady, they share tender breakfasts and suppers, rub noses and just generally behave adorably. But, she only appears early morning and evening and that leaves a whole lot of time for Dutchy to romance the other girls.

The competition, as I've said, can learn a lot from Mr. Romance. He manages to make his rounds with all the ladies. Some of the females stick to one territory. The silver, fox female never seems to go north of the porch, or east of the front yard.

I will see her in the back garden or in the rows of palms which comprise our front yard, but never anywhere else. There is a rabbit who hangs around that appears to be a hybrid domestic-wild rabbit cross. I believe it's a female. She's very friendly, when she deigns to show herself. There is also a darks sable rabbit that I've only ever see in an area around the Pummelo grapefruit trees around our hose pump. This past spring, partly in a wave of nostalgia for our old nursery days and with a vague idea of selling them, we planted several dozen pots full of seedlings and cuttings.

I often see Lady Wild Rabbit standing up, hands politely folded in front of her, eating the grapefruit leaves, or nibbling weeds growing from the sides of the pots, but, I've never seen her anywhere else. Dutchy makes regular visits to her. She seems to be the aggressor, which for Dutchy is not the usual case.

They Grow Up So Fast

Chickens do grow up fast. As I've Mentioned in commercial egg facilities a hen's egg laying career is unmercifully short. This doesn't mean they don't lay eggs as they age, they just lay fewer and when you lay fewer eggs you are no longer useful.

An old hen, like Henley can still lay eggs. We like to think that several of the chicks we see with combinations of Henley's reddish buff color are her legacy. There's one particular white hen with just Henley's color of splotches on her back and wing feathers. She was one of the first hatch offs this spring when we started our repopulating program. It's nice to see our old friends live on in their descendants.

Fainting Hen Turkey

Wild Things

Sometimes we sit out in the early evening and count our blessings for all the beautiful animals we see. One evening last summer, we saw eleven deer come out of the woods, one by one, and then make their way across the field. When we put out corn, during times when there is some reason for a lack of vegetation, some of the does and younger bucks will get as close as thirty feet from my chair.

Sometimes the domestic poultry, wild turkeys, rabbits, squirrels and deer will peaceably congregate for a chance at the corn. As much as I love them, deer are a curse and a blessing as they will wreak destruction on any plant they like to eat.

About four years ago we went out of town for a few days and came back to almost eighty rose bushes chewed down to half their size. A little nibbling probably wouldn't hurt, but they yank on them while they chew and since roses have shallow roots, sometimes the damage will slowly kill them.

They can also strip and eventually kill any tropical hibiscus variety. Around here, they leave the cold, hardy hibiscus Rose of Sharon alone. I had the idea of planting a tropical garden out back a few years ago. It was a good laboratory for discovering what deer did and did not like to eat.

Deer don't eat bananas, birds of paradise, plain bottlebrush, bougainvillea, palms, Angel Trumpets, hydrangeas, lilacs, crape myrtles, Cassias or pineapples. Strangely, they don't like palm fronds, though goats love them. Aside from the hibiscus and roses, they demolish magnolias, ti plants, mulberries and sometimes citrus trees. They can also demolish any vegetable garden.

We fight an uphill battle against animals and bugs when we try to grow things. The summer the Royal Palm turkeys were teenagers, we decided to plant a good size tomato and pepper garden. All poultry will scratch up and destroy young plants, so this can be a challenge.

The act of tilling the soil or watering brings fresh bugs to the surface. We knew we had to fence the tomatoes in, so we put up four foot of wire about 20 x 60 feet and planted beefsteak, heirloom, yellow and pear shaped tomatoes, along with several varieties of peppers. To have any tomatoes, we had to put wire over the top and crawl on our hands and knees to harvest them, not fun.

Turkeys and ducks eat lots of plants that chickens won't. Chickens do most of their damage through scratching and destroying sod or young roots, not actually eating plants. Turkeys seem to like tomatoes better than anything else. That year someone gave me several pounds of cherry tomato seeds, thinking they were too old to be any good. I just raked them into a fenced area and when the tomatoes began to ripen, I took the fence down. Those tomatoes provided the turkey's with their favorite treat and gave us several weeks of laughs watching them. They would chase each other round and round, trying to steal tomatoes from each other.

Sometimes, the animals catch a break. About every five years, around here, there's an overabundance of Live Oak acorns. The tannin in these acorns makes lots of little dogs sick, though Tea Cup

could scarf up at least a dozen before she could be stopped, and she never got sick from them.

While lots of oaks have bitter acorns that even squirrels don't want, bumper Live Oak crop years are like extended Christmas dinner to deer and squirrels. These years hunters have a heck of a time luring deer onto baited corn fields, at least until the acorns are gone. Once our acorns were gone, they moved on and we didn't see another deer all winter.

In the Beginning

Many years ago I went to high school in Tampa. We lived out here by then, but the high school for Land O Lakes was over twenty miles away in Dade City. Eventually it was more convenient for my family to drop me off at Chamberlain High, a half mile from their office, than to have to come all the way to Dade City if I got sick, or missed the bus.

This was in the seventies, a strange crazy time. Many students were involved in anti-war and other protest movements and some were deep into experimentation with drugs. One of the crazy things about this time when you could get an excused absence, just to stay in a gas line for your parents, was that all high schools, I knew of, had designated smoking areas scattered throughout the school grounds. I took several business courses in an annex next to the ROTC and several other specialty classes.

A mix of students would congregate in the covered walkway before and after class, some to smoke, some just to kill time. One day, for some reason a fairly diverse group began debating what we would do when we graduated?

I don't know what actually happened. There was the usual variety of desires and ambitions. Lawyer, actor, artist, veterinarian and then there were those who were in ROTC, the specter of Viet Nam hung heavy over many of them, especially the boys. I only knew one thing.

When we moved out to Land O Lakes, I felt I had found paradise and come home. I had a horse and we spent long, lazy summer days lounging around the lakes and trying to learn various skills like water skiing.

Without even thinking about the law, which was my families preferred profession for me, or something in art or fashion, which were my preferred fields of study, I knew what I wanted to do. Without even thinking, I answered that I wanted to live in the country and find a way to make a living there. I may as well have said I wanted to be an arsonist. What in the world could you do there to make a living? What is there to do for fun? Bear in mind as most kids had vague notions of making it big in New York or LA, or at least living out some version of a big city dream, what I proposed sounded like a nightmare.

It would have been nice to have had a big cattle ranch, but we had what we had with the grove and nursery, I think we did all we could with it. Still, all good things must come to an end. Nothing lasts forever.

It was hard work, almost three hundred sixty five days a year, but, there were good things about it too. In time, several things, made it impossible to continue. Even though we had learned to deal with stiff, almost brutal, competition from big box retailers, most especially the one you can imagine, our property was due to be changed forever.

We stayed in the game by doing things like planting bare root citrus trees and growing them out ourselves, when Wal-Mart's retail price became less than the price we could buy them for wholesale. We also specialized in more exotic tropicals, many we grew ourselves. It was quite a lot of work for two or three people, but, it was satisfying to hold our own and survive against the big guys. We didn't have enough land to make money selling to a wholesaler, so after the mid 80's freezes knocked most of the grove to the ground, we planted lots of different varieties of fruit, that we could sell, retail, but, at reasonable price to the public.

Any variety that could be sold before January was a plus, because there was usually a big Thanksgiving and Christmas rush. Christmas freezes have occurred, but the most likely time for a freeze was January and the first two weeks of February, so you want to pick as much as you can before then.

Calamity

Here, the weather is warm, but not for every night of every year. It's possible to be in the low 70's one afternoon and the next night have the temperatures drop into the 20's. In the late 90's, we had already had some bad nights the previous two years, but we seldom faced anything this bad. We drug out the disgusting, dirty grove heaters and put them around the most valuable trees. A lot of the potted plants in the nursery were laid down and covered, but, the best anecdote to cold is ice.

If ice forms and is left alone, it's temperature will sink to the lowest temperature of the air surrounding it. If fresh water keeps running on the ice, the temperature stays at 32 degrees, harms very few things. Our sprinkler system was a homemade affair with Rain Bird sprinklers mounted on eight foot railroad ties. All you have to do is lay the plants down, so the branches don't break and run the water. Everything should be fine. There's only one problem, when the temperature goes below thirty two degrees early in the night and gets down below twenty seven or twenty eight degrees, the water in the sprinklers freezes.

That's why people who grow anything in Central Florida don't dislike cold weather, we hate it. On nights like this, strawberry farms run massive and efficient sprinkler systems, as do winter vegetable farmers. It doesn't work as well with citrus, because the weight of the ice can break the branches and harm or kill the trees.

I don't know what they do at the big farms where you see the sprinklers going, but our sprinklers start to freeze up when it gets super cold. We devised a very unpleasant way to fix them.

You have to heat a lot of water, bundle up, put the water in pump sprayers and go out and spray the hot water on the sprinklers to get them going again. As you might expect, when the sprinkler head comes back on, you get wet. Since you're also walking around on slippery ice, the chance of injury, especially if you're as clumsy as I am, is fairly high. You can also get a really bad cold. This time it didn't work so well, it was so cold that year we just couldn't keep up with the rate the sprinklers were freezing. Several hours later it didn't matter, the electricity went out and pumps don't run without electricity. Once the ice melted most of the nursery had turned to mush.

We were effectively out of business for the time being, but we still had a lot to do. First, along with my husbands' sister Barbara and her husband Bill, we picked a semi load of oranges that we could sell before they fell off the trees. Then we began cutting the plants back and waited to see if any of them could be salvaged. They couldn't. There was more bad news, but, this had been a possibility for a long time.

The state and the county had been planning to take out the wide curve in the highway, in front of the grove, for years. In the meantime, we'd bought my husband's Uncle Paul's old house and fifteen acres, across the old hard road, that ran behind the grove. We were already saddled with the payments when everything froze.

On top of that, the state was going to use Eminent Domain to force my sister in law's family off their property across the highway and take away our highway frontage when they straightened the curve. The specter of this was effectively spoiling the chance for a successful reopening.

The Tower

We tend to be skeptical about a lot of things. When you've been in business for a while, you meet a lot of people who want to sell you something, others, who want you to sell something for them, and,

still others who want to offer you a once in a lifetime investment opportunity that will set you up for life!

One day in the spring of 1997, we were working out back in the green house. We'd been doing some landscaping to get by and growing some small ornamentals, while getting the grove back in shape. A car parked on the old road and a man in a suit and string tie, carrying a briefcase walked up the driveway. He was polite and businesslike. He already knew we owned the property across the old road. He said he represented one of the major cell phone companies and that our other property would be an ideal spot for a cell phone tower. We took his card and said we'd think about it, momentarily thinking he was a seminar salesman or something.

Before he got to the end of the drive, we'd changed our mind. What did we have to lose? We could sure use the money; we might lose our other property if we didn't have a steady way to make the payment. The offer was legit and after zoning was obtained, they built it and finally we had something that could help us make the mortgage.

Making a Move

I'm making my way back to the animals. My father in law passed away in 1999. He had never wanted to sell the grove and he didn't like Uncle Paul's side of the road, that's why he'd sold it to him in the first place.

He thought like a farmer. Paul's land was too low and swampy in parts for very many acre of grove or other farming, even parts of the cow pasture would flood some years. The other part was high, sandy and infertile. The same type of land he had deemed a bad investment back in the 50's when he turned down cheap lots in north Hillsborough County. A few years later, the University of South Florida, and everything that went with it, was built on the same spot. Some people made a lot of money, but he had passed.

We liked it though and as the road project got nearer, Grandma decided we would sell and divide the money three ways, between my husband, his sister and herself. His sister would eventually move to a seven acre property about three miles south, in Hillsborough County. Grandma and our oldest daughter would live in Paul's old house until it sold and we would live further back about three hundred feet from the road.

We had some nice hens and roosters, a good assortment of sizes and types. Some we had bought at the Sunday afternoon farm auction up in Darby. They sell everything there, from incubators and farm implements to small farm animals. They sell poultry, goats, sheep, even the odd calf or donkey. It's usually pretty crowded with sellers, buyers and some who just come to watch. It's sort of fun if you're not stuck all afternoon waiting for your lot to come up for sale, or waiting to get paid.

Moving the Flock

Once we sold the property, we knew we'd have to move the chickens across the road. There was a nice aluminum barn on the north corner, we put in poles suitably high off the ground to be roosts and we also put in feeders and waterers. We couldn't wait to bring them over.

When we bought the property in the mid 90's, there hadn't been a full time human presence on the property since my husband's cousin had moved away several years before.

We were there several times a week, mowing and planting and clearing, but that, aside from the tower construction was the only human presence on the land in a long time. During this time, the predators had felt encouraged to run amok.

We were so excited about our move that straight away we made plans to fence about an acre of the pine woods behind the house for a turkey pen. We put a sheet metal roosting house inside it and proceeded to buy some turkeys. We thought it would be pleasant and though we hadn't seen the Royal Palm breed yet, turkeys are attractive in their way and most of our family like the eggs. A friend of ours from Thailand gave us two ducks and we put them in with the turkeys, thinking that would be the safest place for them.

Meanwhile back at the chicken house, hens were beginning to mysteriously vanish. All was not well in the poultry world, but, we were about to meet one of our favorite rooster's of all time.

Mr. White

We were lucky to have the tower to pay the mortgage on the property, since the nursery had frozen, but late in the 90's we figured we might as well remodel and rent out Uncle Paul's house. In an experience almost any landlord has gone through, our first renters, after a long period of nonpayment, finally moved. We felt a little burned by the landlord experience, but needed the money, so we saddled up for another try.

The new family was excellent tenants, but, they wanted to buy a house and the house was not zoned for livestock. It was lucky timing. They wanted to move right about the time Grandma needed the house. Our tenant had one big handsome white rooster and a really nicely made coop. We agreed to keep him.

At the time we moved, we had a number of roosters who were more physically stunning than Mr. White, which was what we called the new guy. Probably the most imposing was one was a dead ringer for Mr. Orpington. There were big reds and blacks and multi-colored roosters of several varieties, but, no white ones.

Curiously, these roosters always got along pretty well. They had all grown up in a place where Brownie getting out of his fence and scaring them into the trees, or the eaves of the tractor barn, was the scariest thing they had to face.

At first things went well, aside from a few disappearing hens. We felt we should do some research and find out what varieties of hens would make their nests above the ground where it was safer, and to restock with them when we absolutely needed to.

On Muddy Pond

In the meantime, as many people who move to a new place are, we were filled with plans for home improvement projects. We decided to put in an ornamental goldfish pond. We went out and saw some models and looked up different designs on the internet, did our homework, bought our supplies and went to work. When

we were done, it looked nice. We knew about raising fish and we had shade and proper food for them. We knew that they faced some threat from predators, but, since they were right behind the house where we could keep an eye on them, we hoped we would be able to keep them safe. It looked nice. We landscaped around it and hoped our medium sized goldfish would grow into truly impressive adults.

Like the hens before them, the goldfish began to disappear. We suspected it was a raccoon, so we covered the pond in the evening and wet the ground around it so we might be able to identify the tracks of the predator. Several nights went by and no tracks appeared and no goldfish died. One afternoon, we were out a little later than usual and it was already dark when we got home. There were several fish missing by that time. We covered the little pond, but, noticed we had probably been blaming the wrong predator. There were keeping a constant watch on the pond from the pine trees.

We had identified the enemy, at least, the immediate one. We would have to make sure it was covered very early every evening, if the pretty little fish were going to survive. That was not a problem. The wire we covered it with was narrow, but strong. This way owls or other potential predators would not be able to get at them. We would have to weigh the edges down with rocks, in case something with the ability to drag the wire, like a raccoon tried and pull it off. This plan worked well. We just put it on early, the fish could breathe and they would still be safe.

This went pretty well and pretty easily for over a month. One morning when we went to take the cover off, we were greeted with a creepy sight. There were eight baby Water Moccasins availing themselves of the nice damp spot, since it was the dry season of mid May.

We knew they were Water Moccasins. We'd seen lots of different snake hatchlings before, but, most books on the subjects dwelt more on the looks of the adults than the babies. We'd seen those yellow tipped tails before though. They are the scariest snake we normally come in contact with, here in the wetlands. We have some high dry ground that is more conducive to rattlesnakes and Coral snakes, but, Water Moccasins are the ones we fear the most, because, they seem to have no fear of us.

After this creepy experience, we gave our fish to someone we knew from our old nursery days who had a goldfish pond behind a fence in a nice, safe neighborhood down the road. We pulled out the artificial pond, filled in the cemented edge with sand and eventually put a statue of a manatee and its' baby in the middle, where our pond had stood.

The ordeal of trying to keep something as simple as a small school of goldfish alive, made us realize we were going to have to step up our game if we were ever going to be able to give the birds living on the property an even shot at survival.

After we found the two destroyed nests, we had a few days breather when everyone stayed safe. The roosters got along agreeably well, coming out from their house every morning, running quickly across the small open field and emerging into the relative safety of tree cover.

Chickens of any sort seldom linger in an open field. This is the type of spot where they are most vulnerable to swooping aerial hunters like owls, chicken hawks and the occasional eagle who might be passing through. So whenever they need to negotiate an open space, it seems to be instinct to get across it as quickly as possible. Most of the day, they would go over and hang out in the pines harassing the turkeys behind the fence and occasionally chasing each other. This was boyish hi-jinks in contrast to the way they could behave. In observing them I have noticed that while most roosters are capable of fighting, ambush and even murder, they will behave pretty well when there is plenty of food and things are safe.

If three conditions are favorable, roosters can coexist in fairly large numbers with almost no serious confrontation. This appears to be true for all the chicken breeds I have ever encountered. The three

factors that must be present for peace in the barnyard are a plentiful food supply, a sufficient number of hens and a reasonably secure environment.

Plentiful food supply is not a problem. Chickens should be provided with some kind of fortified chick food when they're little and whole or cracked corn when they get older. They should not be fed so much that they're not motivated to catch the bugs and worms they need for a protein source and the grass and vegetation they need for a varied diet.

If you put out too much corn you not only waste money and resources, but, you also run the risk of attracting what we call varmints. Rats, raccoons, and opossums, just to name a few. At least you'll usually see more birds and squirrels. Poultry and rabbits also love vegetables, so most peelings and wilted lettuce or celery is a treat to them.

There's a constant competition between my husband and I during watermelon season to see who can get hold of the watermelon rinds first. I liked to give them to my daughter's pig, or small slices to the rabbits. We got the pig by default, but he enjoyed the flavor and the activity of melon rinds and I liked to give them to him. Chicken, ducks and turkeys love every part of a melon except the outside shell and will pick them down to the thickness of a sheet of paper in no time flat. That's one of the nice things about having poultry; you don't have to waste any of your peelings or throw away something as bulky as a watermelon rind. The one thing they don't like is banana peels, but goats and pigs adore them. White Ears will run across her pasture for banana peels, but, won't eat bananas, because goats are the pickiest and hardest to please eaters in the barnyard world.

A Word of Warning

A little while ago I remarked that it wasn't animal cruelty to feed a chicken the meat of another chicken. Chickens like all kinds of meat and fish and will seldom turn down cooked meat of any kind. It isn't harmful to chickens to eat meat, but it's dangerous for humans to eat the eggs of chickens who have eaten <u>raw</u> meat. For some reason raw meat eating hens can produce eggs that are unsafe to eat. I have always heard this and a lot of seasoned egg raisers swear by this advice, so it's something I follow and suggest anyone else raising eggs for human consumption, do as well. The uncooked meat or chicken you didn't cook in time, throw it away.

Happy hens, Happy Roosters

Happy hens make for happy roosters. Well, the roosters probably don't care if the hens are happy, but they do care that they're safe and plentiful. As I've mentioned, some roosters are responsible guards and protectors of the hens and some just hang around waiting to jump their bones. Many times I've seen the vanguard roosters standing sentinel close to the edge of the woods, while the hens graze for bugs and seeds. A great hue and cry will arise and everyone will run back toward the chicken house to escape a real, or sometimes, merely perceived threat.

Sometimes a situation arises where there is a disproportionate rooster to hen ratio. That's another reason for fights to break out. Unattached roosters will suddenly begin competing for, or merely jumping on hens that are part of stable rooster and hen groups. This can lead to fights.

A well placed peck will suffice in most cases. Roosters will also take off and chase another rooster they feel has encroached on their territory. Usually in a relatively stress free environment, the flock rooster will just jump up and chase off his potential rival. The Spanish rooster and Shadow have an ongoing relationship of this type and neither one of them is ever close to getting hurt. The Spanish will run Shadow off thirty to fifty feet and he will have to bide his time resting under a bush or something else until he feels he can make another safe approach.

Sometimes if the hen population drops too low and this is always bound to happen as they're "sitting ducks," when they're nesting,

roosters can become fractious. When there are no hens, roosters have nothing to compete for, which means they should have less urge to fight. That would be the sensible reaction.

Roosters like humans aren't always sensible. When there are too few hens, they turn to fighting, perhaps out of boredom, or to achieve a sense of purpose. It might also be that without hens to help them establish their place in the pecking order, they use fighting to establish a different standard of hierarchy. I don't see how anyone could know for sure, but, it's a fact that when there are too few hens, roosters turn to fighting.

Safety First

The third of the big three conditions needed for docile roosters is a relatively low volume of predators. When a rooster calls a general alarm to make a run for it, the outrider roosters run too. There is a seldom, but occasional united front against predators, but it's usually every rooster and hen for themselves once the alarm has been sounded.

I have seen more than one rooster fly up at a rushing predator to create a diversion and give the rest of the flock a chance to make a run for it. I have seen it happen when two, "lost," dogs came out of the woods and two, separate roosters, spaced about twenty feet apart on the vanguard, called the alarm. They both flew up, about four feet off the ground, spurs bared and everyone, the roosters included got away.

When there are multiple threats which raise the levels of stress and fear, sometimes roosters fail to unite against their common enemy. Sometimes, they also turn on each other. Rooster's who have never shown any animosity, or been the slightest bit aggressive can turn on each other in violent, even murderous ways.

War

The hens kept disappearing right after we moved here. We spent one evening gathering up all the eggs and hens we could find and locked them up, in what we thought was the secure chicken barn. The walls were metal. The roof was metal, secure and water tight. The entry gates were six foot chain link fence gates with sheet metal reinforcements so snakes and varmints couldn't climb in. We thought we had done our due diligence and given the roosters, hens and eggs a safe secure place to live at night. But, the threats were about to hit day and night, twenty four hours a day seven days a week.

The turkeys in their bucolic pine grove were the first under attack. We had about one hundred hens and gobblers. We had hand raised them from chicks we ordered from the hatchery. We'd had good luck in keeping almost all of them alive while they grew big enough to go into the enclosure. The idea was to be able to look out into the pine grove and see the turkeys. From a distance the wire was almost as invisible as if they were free. Of course they had a house, which shattered the illusion somewhat, but the overall effect was peaceful and pleasant until the massacres began. The assaults came from raccoons, possums and bobcats, all of whom we had in abundance. We knew it wasn't from predator birds. The pine trees were very close together before they began dying off, and it's difficult for swooping birds like owls and chicken hawks to aim at a target where they can't swoop at an angle. It's not impossible it's just not their preferred way. A night or two after we moved the hens, we woke up in the morning and went to let the chickens and turkeys out. It had been a good night for the chickens, but, not the turkeys. Something had dug under the fence in the back, down by the fish hole and gotten into the house and drug off and killed what we estimated to be fourteen turkeys.

Once predators begin to have some success, it's as if they hang out a sign that says, "Easy Pickings," at your property line. We fixed the fence, which was eight foot tall to make it harder to climb, and hung some broad beam lamps up on the fences and in the trees. We hoped it would spook and disorient the night stalkers. If it kept the turkeys from sleeping soundly, better they were cranky, than they were dinner. It was better than nothing and we stayed up late driving

around to the back and shining a spot light on the fence to make sure nothing was digging under it.

One night down and many more to go before this place belonged to us and not the vast army of predators. We found another destroyed chicken nest. It was so well hidden in the bushes, we only found it because the killer had bent and broken some of the branches she had used as cover. This was what appeared to be the work of a destructive, no good possum.

I know that sounds judgmental, but raccoons, foxes and even chicken snakes eat eggs and then they leave. A raccoon, bobcat or fox might kill the hen and drag her away to eat. They'll eat pretty much all edible parts, with minimal waste. An opossum, on the other hand, may only eat two or three eggs, then break the other eggs. This leaves the mom nothing and makes a smelly mess that's bound to draw the attention of other varmints.

I'm sure it was just a coincidence, but, this one little event seemed to be the catalyst for all hell to break loose. After that, the threats came day and night.

Hens were killed, nests were destroyed and turkeys began to vanish again. Whatever we did, it wasn't enough. Our fantasy of a peaceful place where the birds could live in relative freedom was slipping away, and it seemed as if there was nothing we could do about it. We felt responsible for the situation and resolved to do what we could to fix it.

Junk Yard Dogs

Our oldest daughter had a Chihuahua named Teacup. She'd taken her when she moved to Tampa to go to college. Teacup disliked being alone all day so we enlisted her to help us with our varmint problem. I don't endorse letting dogs run loose. We already had a little run and house for Brownie, so we had another one built for her. Brownie didn't bark much on his own, but he would follow Teacup's lead. Together they sounded very formidable.

We decided our chicken house was too far from the lights and noise of the house. We'd used a building that was already there, because we hate waste and wanted to save money. We couldn't be sure, but, it seemed that the sturdy barn we'd thought would be so safe was just too far out in the open, but with a dangerous line of trees separating it from the industrial property to our north. We made plans to build a new one on the south side of the house, in the oak and pine. This would take time though.

One of the odd things we've found over time is once chickens are free range, if you have several varieties, the genetic possibilities are endless. Like many people, we'd bought the showiest roosters and the fluffiest hens, all purebreds. Like other domesticated animals, poultry varieties reflect human tastes and desires, not the biological objectives of the animals. Wild poultry breeds can still be found in some parts of the world, usually in temperate climates. They are much smaller and lay smaller eggs than domestic birds. Nature breeds infinite variety, but efficient adaptation too. Wild birds adapt to whatever dangers their world throws at them. They're speedy and shrewd, or they'd be extinct.

Contrast small birds that lay small eggs, but have wariness and quick speed with the giant birds that humans have bred for their large breasts, large eggs and showy feathers. We realized that had been part of our problem. We had brought birds for their looks, and some of these guys were huge. If you have to run from predators, the wider and heavier you are, the slower you are likely to be, just like with humans. Over the years as our chickens have crossbred with smaller birds, many of them are quite unique.

We bought a few bantams the next season. We didn't yet realize the hens are so vulnerable, as they resist nesting high to the ground. They're usually the best flyers though and can out fly most predators. The roosters can breed moderate to larger hens and for long periods of time this can increase the diversity of the flock and their level of survival.

Wild Things

We had no experience of wild or feral chickens except from nature shows and seeing them in Key West. We do see wild turkeys almost every day and ducks when we go down to the creek.

Wild turkeys are nothing like domestic turkeys, in looks or behavior. Wild ones are longer and slimmer of body and light for their size, which aids them if they have to run, or fly to safety. They also form different types of families based on taste or need. Some are traditional, one tom multi hen groups. Some have more males, some have equal or greater numbers of females and sometimes two or more hens will even strike out on their own with little ones in tow. They're also what we refer to as, "lone gunmen." These are rogue males who have either lost their flock or been expelled from a flock for one reason or another. Sometimes they are smaller or have a limp or other injury that would make keeping up with the rest of a flock difficult.

It's often a mystery as wild flocks will occasionally accept domestic turkeys that are also slower and want to join the group. Most of these birds are fast, shrewd and have beautiful dark brown feathers. For the first several years we lived here we only saw wild turkeys from a distance. If they thought we were too close, they would fly off. We never harmed them and put out corn in the winter, so eventually we became just part of the scenery to them.

After the big hurricane year when the water receded in the fields, between the house and the forest, the open spaces beside the woods became irresistible to the wild turkeys. I guess that whatever they found in the fields was pretty tasty, especially since there were still so many parts of their territory under water. They fed for hours at a time and as long as we didn't go right up to them, they would let us watch them graze. They became used to seeing us and over the years, they've come to think of us almost as if we were just another sort of bird. This summer when it was raining so much, a female led family of two hens and eleven approximately three month old chicks began poaching corn from the back drive and later appearing to request, and then demand, more. By winter they were less frequent, but still occasional visitors.

We don't interfere with the wild animals in any way, except for feeding them. Acquaintances have occasionally offered to buy our feed in return for being able to use our property as a hunting base, but, even though it amounts to a total of seven thousand acres, the wildlife management area is a fairly narrow strip at some points behind us. There's a nice family neighborhood on the other side to the west. It's just too close, so we don't allow shooting, except for occasional target shooting, or shooting a water moccasin. We can often hear unauthorized shooting out there though, especially during hunting season.

A Little History (I promise it won't be long or too boring)

As you can probably know, parts of Florida have experienced explosive growth, especially since the 1960's. This caused a clash of cultures as well as the inevitable environmental and wildlife habitat problems.

Before World War II, many of Florida's citizens were small farm owners, cattle ranchers or raised some mixture of citrus, small crops and farm animals. Most people associate Florida with beaches or oranges, but, cattle were the driving force behind many a Florida fortune. The reason Florida natives were called by the name "Cracker," was derived from the sound made by the whips on drives that took cattle to the rail hubs. Florida provided most of the beef and a good portion of the other commodities that fed the Confederate forces during the Civil War, though, the state was sparsely populated at the time.

By World War II, Florida still mainly consisted of farms of one sort or another, with Miami, Tampa and Jacksonville being the main small cities. Orlando was then a small farming community.

The War changed everything. Naval bases, Air Force and Army bases, shipyards, airfields and the towns that supported them, grew during, and after the war.

You might know the old expression, "you can't keep them down on the farm," that was indeed the case. A lot of young women who worked in the war industries and young men who'd been off to Europe or the Pacific began to want lives outside of agriculture, with all of its limits and risk. On top of this, lots of the military personnel that had spent time in Florida began to wish they could come back. Breweries, aerospace, banking, the growth of retirement communities and the rise of theme parks and other tourist attractions combined with all the jobs they needed filled, were just some of the new enterprises that helped fuel central Florida's huge population boom.

Water Wars
By the late 1960's, Pinellas county, mainly St. Petersburg and Clearwater and Hillsborough County, mainly Tampa, were running out of the water that could be pumped from under their own ground. Other parts of Florida were facing similar problems, so water management districts and study groups were set up by the state to help find solutions.

Pasco County has a town that is called Land O Lakes for a reason. The county sits on billions of gallons of water our neighbors to the south coveted for their own use. Pasco was sparsely populated and therefore underrepresented on the water boards. Before you knew it, plans for giant well fields were put into execution. Thousands of acres of support preserve were snatched up by the Southwest Florida Water Management District, or Swift Mud as it is known. Lots of people considered them the enemy. A fair number of people had their ponds and wetlands sucked dry, which the authorities then claimed hadn't happened. The value of some people's land was lowered, as certain land uses were restricted in an effort to keep the lands surrounding the well fields free of pollutants. Soon the Cypress Creek Well field in Land O Lakes and the Cosme Odessa field in Odessa were our new neighbors. Much the same thing happened to the sparsely populated states that bordered the Colorado River when California needed their water to fuel its' own postwar expansion.

The Water Wars combined with one man made and one nature made phenomenon were about to change Pasco County forever.

Prior to the early 1970's most of the population of the county was clustered on the Gulf of Mexico, in Port Richey, New Port Richey and Hudson. The county seat was in the east in the prosperous grove and ranch town of Dade City. The large Benedictine monastery and college of St Leo was next door in San Antonio. Caught in the middle was Land O' Lakes, the odd man out as far as political power in the county went.

Interstate 75 developed and an exit was built at Wesley Chapel. US 41 ran north from Tampa through Land O Lakes, just a few miles to the west. This made these the first two places people going north from Tampa came to. State Road 54 connected the two. That was all that was needed to bring disaffected city residents, especially those who were yearning for wide open spaces. Affordable waterfront and a reasonably short commute from their little pieces of suburban/semi-rural heaven were an added lure.

At about the same time the cities began coveting our abundant land and water, there was a slight shift in the weather patterns. It's not that noticeable if you're snug in bed in your centrally heated home, but painfully apparent if you have an orange grove. A lot of the groves in Land O Lakes and north to Dade City were small fifteen to fifty acre family groves, but, some ran into hundreds, even thousands of acres. If they were wiped out by a freeze and had no land in cattle or hardy crops, they needed to sell at least a part of their land to keep going. Some could sell some lake front to fund replanting or just to pay to bulldoze the trees.

Those who wanted to get out of the high risk game of growing had to hire some engineers, build streets and survey residential lots, or small 2 to 10 acre "estates." This was a new phase in the development of our little part of the Sunshine State.

That's how my family moved out here. We'd drive out on Sunday and look at real estate. The more developed parts of Wesley Chapel were rejected by my grandfather because they were pretty low, on land that was prone to flooding. The reasonably priced one-third acre lots on Lake Padgett in Land O Lakes seemed just right. We moved out here around 1970, when there were still only a few hundred people close by. Back then the closest junior high and high schools were around twenty miles away in Dade City. I've never really wanted to live anywhere else.

In a curious footnote, some of the Wesley Chapel home sites that my family worried might flood, faced the opposite problem once the well fields had been pumping at full capacity for a few years. By the late eighties and early nineties, ponds and other wetlands began drying up.

The oddest thing was that hundred year old oaks began to look as if they were rising out of the ground. Common sense and observation led us to believe this was because the water was being depleted. There were lawsuits, but, it's hard to fight city hall, or in this case a regional water authority. The heavily stacked odds say that when you fight the state of Florida and their representative authorities, you will not win. Swift Mud eventually began rotating the well fields and instituted more conservation measures.

The Romance of the Twenty First Century

My favorite chickens, just for beauty and behavior are bantams, the little fellows. We've purchased or accidently acquired a few. They can fly higher and move more gracefully than any other chicken. Unless they are old or injured, they have no problem flying out of an eight to ten foot fence, even if it's too narrow to allow for the takeoff room a bigger chicken needs.

They sometimes seem as if they feel superior to other chickens, because they often stick to themselves socially, though the males will mate with bigger hens and harass bigger roosters.

For over six years we had an alpha, loner, male bantam I called Mr. Grey. He had a silvery-gray chest and a beautiful cream colored mane of feathers around his neck. Since the hens are hard to keep unless they are completely locked up in a chicken house, we have never kept very many at a time.

The prettiest bantam hen I've ever seen came to us several months after Mr. Grey did. I called her French White, because she reminded me of the three French hens in *The Twelve Days of Christmas*. She was really A Japanese White, maybe with a little something else thrown in. She was small, showy, and graceful, though, unfortunately, since she had been a hand raised pet, very tame. She made little cooing sounds like a dove and could do the most amazing thing I have ever seen any chicken do.

While most bantams can fly practically straight up a few feet, and it's always fascinating to see, she could fly so high and so straight that it was like watching an angel ascend into heaven. If I went out under the trees as the chickens were ascending to the different parts of the old twisted oak they preferred, I could watch her ascend virtually straight through a place where two branches made a separation. She

would then climb to the highest roosting point of any of the chickens or turkeys. I thought she deserved the highest spot, for to me, she was like a little queen, or perhaps an angel.

Mr. Grey was a loner, and she was not particularly friendly with any of the other birds, as she had no ties to them. They began to spend all their time together. There were only four other bantam hens around at the time and four other roosters that size. One was a regular Sea Bright. They have pretty geometric patterned feathers that are orangish red with black patterns. He was cussed though; he'd chase you if you went by on the golf cart with your foot hanging off. We'd put him in the fence every few days where he was curiously docile when he was surrounded by bigger birds.

There were also two extremely handsome roosters who must have been identical twins. They had the same geometric design as a Sea bright, but theirs' were black on pale gold. I called them the Golden Boys, I and II.

There was also a very memorable fellow named Clown. He was a Black Spanish, small, with good looking tail feathers and a devilish and somewhat aggressive way about him. He had white flaps of skin on his face and a red skin-beard, something like a turkey's wattle only smaller. The stark red and white contrast suggested his name to me. He would take up with two or three hens occasionally for a few days, but, lacked the patience to follow them out into the fields and pines and circle their perimeter as a guard. He preferred to march up and down the back yard. He would march between the little shaded yard that was Boomer's, to the oaks in front of the chicken house and then back. He'd look for something that he could chase or fly up at, before resuming his determined march up and down the yard.

I've found that it's not good to get too sentimental about chickens and other yard birds, that's why I give them generic names that reflect aspects of their physical looks or personality. Even under the safest and most optimum circumstances, their lifespan is short sometimes, painfully short. Of course I miss them when they're gone. I always hope that the best and brightest of their characteristics will continue on through their children.

Mr. and Mrs.

Mrs. White and Mr. Grey kept exclusive company for quite a time before she vanished. We found her under our big commercial lawnmower, nesting. I don't know why bantam hens don't nest far off the ground. I try to resist ascribing human motives to animals, but, it almost seems their too conceited to hatch eggs laid by other hens in the nest boxes.

The more logical reason seems part biology, part sociology. Bantam hens are tiny compared to some of the domestic hens who have been bred for big breasts or big eggs. A bantam hen like Mrs. White might be able to safely keep a whole clutch of tiny eggs warm, but be only big enough for two or three of the large eggs like you find in the grocery store. If they laid eggs in common nests, or in a raised nest where other hens would co-opt some of the laying space, they wouldn't be able to guarantee they could hatch eggs they can be sure are their own. Also, their small stature seems to guarantee that they are biologically closer to their wild ancestors who tend to be ground nesters.

Bantam hens in my experience won't always associate with large breed hens. The roosters are equally exclusive and I stress this is only my narrow observation. They seem to produce a higher percentage of loners than I've found in other breeds too. They're not exclusive about the hens they will jump on though.

Of seven little roosters we had at the same time for three plus years, four were voluntary loners and the other three accepted constant female companionship only grudgingly. They don't guard very well and they don't support very much. When they attract females it seems very similar to the actions of the groupies who follow rock stars. These girls don't get a whole lot of attention or affection. The little rooster's are just too self absorbed. That was one reason I

found the Mrs. White, Mr. Grey pairing so fascinating. He never even looked at another hen in her company and would circle around looking for threats whenever they wandered further than the immediate back yard area.

No hybrid baby Mrs. White and Mr. Grey baby chicks hatched from this particular nesting, for one morning there she was side by side with Mr. Grey scratching tiny little holes in the hydrangea beds. We looked under the lawn mower, and her nest was empty. I had no way of knowing how many eggs there had been, or what ate them, but, I was disappointed just the same.

Romeo and Juliet never let up. The only problem they ever encountered was the occasional interruption by Golden Boy I. He would appear out of nowhere and sidle up to her, though he never directly ambushed her. He would come right up to them and then quickly scoot off before Mr. Grey could pop him. He would seem to, "accidently," run into them two or three, then three or four times a day. Mrs. White didn't appear to do anything to encourage him, but there just wasn't a whole lot of bantam hen competition out there, so he seemed to be signaling his availability. Usually when a rooster makes a move for an attached hen, it seems more a power play than about the hen. It's kind of like the intruder rooster is sticking his tongue out and taunting the other rooster with his ability to make a move. These two always seemed more affectionate and personal together because one couple pairings that last all day, every day, are fairly unusual among free range poultry.

Henley liked the single life, but for a long time she would graze with an unattached, medium sized white rooster for about two hours a day. She never joined a group, she liked to do her own thing, but, she maintained good relations with the other birds and had a few hen friends she visited with. For a while she did seem to have a standing, daily date with this attractive younger man. This relationship lasted for about four months.

Even with the daily intrusions of Golden Boy, nothing could ruffle the feathers of our principle chicken romance. They even roosted side by side. Several months later, Mrs. White nested again. This time after twenty eight days, she had perfect success. Two buttercup yellow chicks were born. She never spent another moment alone with Mr. Grey as long as she lived.

What happened?

For a few days Mrs. White, as a good mama hen should, stayed alone with her chicks, furiously protective of anything or anyone coming near them. I could get pretty close, but, I didn't push it. I was curious about which parent would be the one the chicks looked like and whether they would be hens or roosters, or one of each. The mystery was why all of a sudden dad was persona non grata.

Their behavior hadn't changed prior to her nesting, nor had her attitude to him appeared to change. While she was nesting he had behaved himself and stayed true to his previous "I want to be alone attitude." He'd made no rude overtures to other hens, at least that I could see and how would she know if he had? What could have happened to the most exclusive and seemingly romantic relationship I'd ever seen between two chickens?

The plot thickened when two weeks later as the chicks had grown stronger, Mrs. White did something totally unexpected.

On that morning, Mrs. White and the chicks were with Golden Boy I and from that day on, they were together. She had the same exclusive relationship with him she had had with Mr. Grey. The only difference was now there were chicks in tow. As they grew, it became apparent that they were going to be very similar, but not exactly like their father. They were a slightly shorter then their dad and slightly plumper and wider in the breast. They looked ninety percent Mr. Grey, but the ten percent Mrs. White made them even more attractive in my eyes. His cream colored neck feathers were a shinier and fluffier white and his grey breast was lighter and more silvery on his

sons. They grew into the most handsome little roosters I think I'd ever seen.

Their little blended family seemed totally devoted to each other. They kept to themselves and seldom interacted with other animals.

What happened? How could a little hen seemingly so devoted to one rooster before her eggs hatched become so completely devoted to a new rooster after the chicks were born? She had never encouraged him when he had approached them or even seemed to pay him any attention.

Mr. Grey seemed to bear no resentment. He has never taken up with another hen and mainly just makes his rounds in a several hundred foot loop through the back yard out toward the chicken house, around the fence and back.

This year, we lost some of the flock to old age and some to the usual suspects. We stopped taking eggs for a while, so we could let the hens hatch out a new generation. We would put around six to ten chicks in the little play yards once they had grown big enough to be out of the heat lights. Grown hens will stop by, looking for spilled corn. They couldn't care less about chicks they're not sure they hatched.

The strangest nursery viewer is Mr. Grey. He will spend thirty minutes or more intently staring into the little yards. He will occasionally walk up and down the fences with the turkey boys and the other unattached males, watching the older, pre teenagers too. It almost seems as if in the twilight of his life, for he is five, that he has finally redeveloped a need for companionship. Perhaps he is looking for a new Mrs. White, or perhaps he's just bored. He has even acquired an unusual choice of buddy.

Every afternoon during the hottest part of the day he and his buddy hang out in the palms around the porch, or occasionally under the john boat out in the pines. In the old days they would have called these boys, Mutt and Jeff for his friend is huge and he's tiny.

His friend is a semi outcast, half Aracuna, white rooster with a funny mangled red comb that falls forward over his eyes. Even though he isn't accepted willingly by any of the mini flocks or unattached hens, he's still managed to father several impressive successors. One of his sons, we believe, is the big white and buff rooster we like to think is his son with Henley. Despite the boy's temporary hijinx chasing the golf cart, he's a beautiful rooster and we have high hopes that as a third generation part Aracuna he will be able to gain the social acceptance his father and grandfather were denied.

He is his funny headed dad's only other buddy. They can often be seen under one of the big oak trees shooting the breeze at least twice a day. He always cruises by the little kindergartners in a hopeful way, just like the other boys.

The Twins

The little nuclear family which consisted of Mrs. White, Golden Boy and Mr. Grey's twin sons continued in bucolic peace for quite a while with no drama or disruption of any kind. They were always together, the four of them, all day long.

Perhaps that was the reason for her abrupt shift from one rooster to the other. Mr. Grey was a loner his whole life except for his brief

sojourn with her. Maybe she felt Mr. Grey was not good father mate-rial, or that he would tolerate the boys, but, not be there in the case something happened to her before they were grown.

I remember a line from the movie *Indiana Jones and the Last Crusade*. Harrison Ford has only one choice to pick the chalice used in Christ's Last Supper. One of the Templar guards of the grail tells him he must, "Choose wisely." He did, and Mrs. White did as well.

Over a year went on with the four of them together. Little hens would try to attach themselves to the handsome young twins as they matured, but, usually after a few days of watching the vanity parade which took up most of their day, they would wander off shaking their little beaks.

The boys were mainly interested in hopping up on stumps and doing a pose off. They would strike a standard repertoire of poses as if to say, "Do you think I'm sexy?" They puff up their chests and arch their necks and make themselves look a little bigger than they really are. They were irresistible, to each other. Their total absorption with themselves was their biggest obstacle to having successful relation-ships with hens. That's not to say they didn't jump on the hens, they just didn't stay.

Several different hens over the years have braved their indiffer-ence to hang around with them and try to coax some sense of rooster responsibility out of them. They're only tolerated, not cared for. The last one was a pretty little golden Sea Bright. She had a sweet and tame disposition and she hung around the family for about three months before she became fed up and voluntarily went to live with some other hens by the chicken house.

I've rambled on too long, mainly because the next part is hard to write. Some hens sit on nests and some don't. Those that do can postpone sitting, but eventually they will do it again. The same held true for Mrs. White.

After about fourteen months she made a nest in an upturned egg crate under a roofed area that shaded some rabbit hutches and the lawnmower. It was behind a stack of plywood and lattice, so it was nearly invisible to the naked eye. She'd made a nice one, lots of pine needles for depth, with a nice layer of soft leaves over them so it would be soft to sit in. It didn't last a week and then she was back with the clan for a few days. She wouldn't go back to the same nest, but soon she vanished again.

I looked for her. She was up in the undercarriage of an old camper truck we used for storage. It must have seemed a clever hiding place, for it took me a while to find her. I discreetly checked her every day and for about two weeks everything went fine. The next day when I looked underneath the truck my heart sank. Where she had been there were leaves and needles scattered in a circle. I hunted Golden Boy and the twins and they were alone.

She'd had the keenest sense of rooster worthiness I've ever seen, for Golden Boy never went more than a few feet away from the twins, for years.

Pretty roosters are a pleasure to watch, even for all their vanity. I always cherished the twins as two of my favorites, mainly because of her. They like little extra bits of fruit, just as much as anyone else. Even so, they never acknowledge me or act as if they are aware of my existence when I give them something.

I don't know what happened, but one day late in the fall, there was Golden Boy, his brother Golden Boy II and one twin. I thought other twin might be down at the fence checking out the future kids, but, he was nowhere to be found. We'll never know what happened, though I'm sure Golden Boy would have fought to the death to protect him, if he could.

The Gladiators

In the ten plus years since we moved here we've planted hundred of trees and bushes. We've planted several hundred Queen Palms, grapefruit and mulberry trees and every kind of flower and bulb we wanted to try. Most of the palms are planted as decoration, but we also have several spots where they are planted to sell someday.

When we moved here however there was nothing but the pines, the trees in the woods, and one L shaped planting of thirty navel orange trees Uncle Paul had planted. Since we didn't live here and still worked full time, watering anything would be a challenge. Since much of the area we would want to plant is in what we call high sandy it would probably have been a complete waste of time.

The lack of small bushes was part of our initial problem in providing a safe habitat for the chickens. They use branch cover for a whole host of things. Hens duck under bushes to escape male attention and roosters use them to avoid getting pounced on by their enemies. They also use lawn chairs, picnic tables, vehicles and anything else they can duck under for the same reason. Especially in unfamiliar places, chickens stay out of the middle of open fields to avoid the possibility of a swooping attack from above.

That was one of the first things I noticed about the roosters who evaded the predators and stayed alive in the months after we moved here. In the morning the big roosters would run as fast as their legs could carry them across the two hundred feet of open field to the relative safety of the pine trees.

There had been fewer open spaces at our old place and we were always so busy working I had never noticed this behavior before. One day, Mr. White and a huge Rhode Island Red began to scrap.

Full blooded domestic chickens don't engage in protracted violent episodes very often, they have been bred to be docile. Unusual circumstances had forced this show down. A placid nature is a desirable trait in the barnyard and almost always personal animosity is quickly acted on with more show than force.

The males do go through some interesting motions when they're, "fighting." They jut their necks forward, puff their neck feathers out and jump about a foot off the ground as they kick their feet at their opponent. The neck feather fluffing is fascinating to see, for their feathers look like the circular heavily, ruffled collars you see in Elizabethan portraits. Usually, three of four of these displays suffice to satisfy male pride and they grudgingly go back about their business. They also chase one another and try to tag their adversary with their beak. This is where the bushes come in handy. The other effective way to avoid getting popped is to be small enough to outrun your adversary or fly into a tree where a bigger chicken can't easily follow.

The most sustained effort I thought Mr. White and the big red one could muster would be a few showy grand jette leaps and maybe a twenty foot chase.

I was wrong. Whatever had gone wrong between these two boys wasn't going to be mended by a quick blowing off of steam. I was worried if they came to true blows, Mr. White would be a goner, as he was smaller and appeared to be older. Mr. White surprised me. There were only a couple of leaping displays and when they landed

Mr. White took off after Big Red and chased him into the pines. His purpose seemed to be to wear the other rooster down.

There were no little bushes to duck under just the big pines to hide behind. He would get a little break and then Mr. White would give chase again. At first I tried getting between them as they were weaving through the pines, but, they were too fast for me and I didn't have enough hose to go that far and try to break it up. I was by myself that morning and I was scared of the pines.

If you saw them now, almost half of them felled by saw or pine borers, you wouldn't understand. Then, they were dark and thick and there were about twenty years of felled needles on the ground beneath them. That's was what really scared me. Now we have to worry about falling limbs, then I worried about the numerous poison snakes that could be in pine needles that hadn't been disturbed in years. Even a big snake can glide under thick pine needles, rendering it invisible. It might just be a chicken snake taking a nap, but in a place undisturbed for so long, the odds were it could be something dangerous.

Mr. White wasn't giving up. He would let Big Red rest for a few minutes and then he'd give chase again. This went on for about three hours. It seemed to me that Mr. White should have worn out at the same rate as Big Red, he was older. He seemed to have some kind of deep grudge that gave him extra energy. By two in the afternoon, Big Red had collapsed. I'd gone inside for a while, as it seemed there was nothing I could do by myself. When I came back out after lunch, Mr. White was tired, but, triumphant. His rival had been run to death. Mr. White hadn't touched a feather on him, yet, he killed him just the same.

Where's Iron Eyes Cody When You Need Him?

If you live somewhere where it looks like you're in the country, but, you're just outside a big city, you've probably experienced the same kind of exasperating annoyance we have. We'll spend an hour picking up trash on both sides of the road, up to the bridge and back, in front of our house. We filled one and a half twenty five gallon nursery pots with beer cans, beer bottles, liquor bottles, little plastic shot bottles, paper sacks, cigarette packs and fast food containers, plus paper and plastic bags of every sort. That's not the worst or most unusual things we've ever found. There are also tree branches and abandoned furniture sometimes, but that's a problem for the county to pick up.

My husband believes the high incidence of alcohol paraphernalia is an unintended consequence of the, "Open Container Law." I don't know. There are trash receptacles at the store at the end of the road and the Walgreen's on the other end. There is also a bench down the road which has a trash can beside it, so there is no excuse for littering. People can be rude, dirty and inconsiderate.

There was some debate a few years back when it was found that Singapore has a law which allows flogging those convicted of littering. Well, I don't know about anything that harsh, but after the umpteenth time you've picked up the trash, you begin to think some kind of penalty might be a pretty good idea.

There was a scene in *Mad Men* where the gorgeous Draper family went on a lovely picnic. It was beautiful. It was a real Kodak moment and that was the ulterior motive for the picnic, a Kodak account. When Don takes the kids to the car, Betty cleans up the picnic things by shaking the cups and plates on the tablecloth into the breeze.

I don't really know what this scene was meant to say, but, sometime in the 60's anti-littering ad campaigns showed up. The best, most memorable one featured Native American, actor Iron Eyes Cody getting a tear in his eye as he surveys a garbage strewn scene. Around the same time seat belt laws and seat belt awareness got the same media treatment as the anti-littering campaign. Many years later we have taught most people to wear seat belts, but, from where we sit, the anti-littering campaign was either an utter failure, or they need to do it again.

They're so Vain

Duck looked like any other Muscovy duck, except for his flipped up wings. We had a dilemma with the Royal Palm turkeys. When we let them wander free, they would vanish completely, or become a trail of feathers that surely had not ended well. If we kept them locked up in the chicken yard they became listless and dirty and acted like they were miserable. I'd never seen poultry so miserable in captivity, most of them just adapt and form new sorts of social groups. Since there were only two males and three females left, we decided to let them go free, as clearly that was their wish. We would just have to keep our fingers crossed and hope for the best.

Within hours the two toms acted like their old selves. With these four it had always been like retired couples out for a drive. The two

hens stayed together and the two toms were usually not far away, but they weren't really paying the girls much attention. The only times they really acted like they cared was purely for their own gratification. They would walk by the ladies, fan out their tails and turn their impressive wattles blue and red, while they brushed their wings against the ground making the swooshing sound that's supposed to make the girl's swoon. They usually couldn't care less. Turkeys are completely different than chickens. Chickens can lay and hatch eggs anytime of the year. They lay a lot fewer eggs when it's raining or cold, but, they can still lay eggs twelve months a year.

Turkeys on the other hand lay once a year, normally in the late spring. The rest of the year, they kind of roll their eyes at the boys and go about their business of grazing and making soft chatter that sounds like a whispered gobble. As to the grazing, turkeys can munch down grass just like a cow and they don't stop there.

Chickens destroy by scratching. The ground in the pine grove that was as smooth as a sidewalk when we moved here became a bumpy, hole-filled, scratched up mess after a couple of years of manic bug hunting. The main reason chicken's scratch is to look for bugs, though it sometimes seems as if they scratch just to make potholes and destroy vegetation. If you want to clear a spot of sod or weeds, just corral chickens on the spot and they'll do the hoeing and weeding for you, very quickly. They don't destroy many plants by eating them though.

Turkeys eat everything. They can graze a lawn, literally to death. If you put out grass seed, or even patchy sod, they will destroy it before it has a good chance to get established. All vegetables, except asparagus, they will also destroy. The same holds true with some herbs, especially chives. Bugs won't touch marigolds, but turkeys and rabbits will rip them to shreds. The only small plants safe from turkey grazing are ones that are toxic like periwinkles or fibrous stemmed like impatiens. They just don't seem to like them, though rabbits will occasionally graze them.

Our two male turkeys are somewhat less destructive. They have a full time occupation parading up and down, fanning their tails and turning their heads red and blue. One male is dominant. He has head skin that falls over his right eye and extends about five inches. He has double the neck skin of the other male.

The other male has a beard that is triple the length and width of the other male, therefore I call them Skin and Beard. Skin trumps beard in the turkey world for Beard must groom Skin's head and neck on demand. There are other indicators of dominance like directing movement by, "siding." The dominant male will walk along beside the other and slowly shove, with a slightly extended wing, his companion in the direction he decides is best.

The Toms would probably have been all right, if they hadn't been so vain. Duck never had a problem with the lady turkeys. They could eat or mingle side by side with no problem.

Once he saw the males puff their tail feathers and try to strut, they were doomed to a life of being chased down and harassed by a guy that wasn't going to tolerate that kind of thing. If it hadn't been so funny, we would have probably separated them, because Duck could run just fast enough to grab one or two strategic tail feathers and ruin the look of their tails, but they grow back quickly. Domestic turkeys are slow and rather clumsy due to their big breasts. Show breeds like the Royal Palms aren't much faster than a duck whose curled wings make him run with a limp.

One odd thing about Duck's attitude to the turkeys was that he was never roused against them until they fanned out their tails and did their skin color change trick. Perhaps he saw it as a challenge, or was jealous of their flashy plumage.

Duck had a similarly violent reaction to the twins when they did their little pose offs on the pine tree stumps. Since the twins were small and lightning fast, Duck was all chase and no catch whenever he caught them in a pose off. For the most part Duck and the Twins hung out in different areas. They were usually only a few hundred

feet apart, but, it kept them out of his main orbit, which was being the shadow and behavior monitor of the Toms. His behavior was so unlike anything we'd ever seen before that we made up theories and jokes about it.

Duck had been raised pretty much as an only duck. The lady who took him in didn't have any other ducks. He'd probably seen the occasional few out on the creek, from a distance. He'd probably never been given proper instruction in duck behavior, so he just winged it.

We joked that Duck's reaction was a combination of sexual frustration, jealousy or a little bit of both. We considered getting a girl duck to calm him down. We rejected the idea because often a romantic obsession in a middle aged chicken can lead a rooster, or duck and their intended into danger. Romance often seemed to leave them with impaired judgment. We didn't want to risk losing him, so we just left him alone.

He must have been Lonely

After the massacres of the birds when we first moved here, we didn't really host many poultry for a while, except our adopted, friend Mr. White. For well over three years, he roosted on our porch rail, right by our back door. The natural desire for sexual companionship and romance seemed to have been his doom.

We let some folks we knew bring a big, safe chicken coop full of hens and put it in the pines when they moved into a neighborhood that wasn't zoned for chickens. Mr. White so enjoyed flirting with the hens that he would return to his roost later and later each evening.

One night just at dark, when a rainstorm came up out of nowhere, he failed to show up at all. He was obviously killed in full view of the hens. He only made it a few feet from the fence. We didn't want to upset Duck's successful apple cart, so we resisted the quite natural urge to give him some duck-like companionship.

Rabbit Redux

Once there were four baby rabbit brothers and sisters and several months later, they were all still here. There was then an interesting rabbit day. For as much as three or four weeks straight we never know if the fourth rabbit was still with us, for, he or she, only made appearances about that often. About a week later we took some trash out to the dumpster, looked back into the grapefruit trees and saw all three spotted rabbits and their solid sibling, together, enjoying an evening nibble in the tall grass.

The same evening, I'd been running a soaker hose on my husband's guava bushes. They'd just finished fruiting so they looked pretty rough, that's why they were getting extra water and care. I looked over towards the tower and saw Dutchy on the outside of the fence and a male spotted rabbit on the inside of the fence. They were about three feet apart and furiously digging. I thought they must be after some kind of tasty root, but, they only dug a little and then moved a few inches closer together and began again. After repeating the maneuvering and furious digging six times they were only a few inches apart. Suddenly, they both leapt into the air and crashed into each other about ten inches off the ground. They moved so fast that I could hardly see the blows struck. Dutchy came up with a small patch of spotted rabbit's hair in his mouth and, what I perceived to be a look of satisfaction, on his face. The spotted fellow then beat a hasty retreat.

One day he'll be larger than Dutchy and if he has any speed or cunning, he'll be able to take his revenge.

Don't Judge Our Ways and We Won't Judge Yours

Florida was only sparsely settled by Europeans for centuries, though Native Americans were here in robust numbers, until they were depleted by conquest and disease. Once the plantation system was established, runaway slaves called Maroons joined the Seminoles as they were pushed further and further south.

There were forts, small harbors and fishing villages in Florida, but, few voluntary settlers braved the harsh combination of heat, vector born disease and wild storms to become permanent settlers until the first few decades of the 19th century.

The explosion in demand for oranges and other citrus, combined with higher demand for beef, caused what was for a very under populated place, a population explosion. There was even an expansion of cotton farming into north and central Florida. The newcomers without much built up resistance, died of mosquito born diseases in astonishingly high numbers.

Fast forward to today. In Pasco County we have what are called Mosquito Control Commissioners. These are elected, part time citizen overseers of the helicopter spraying, truck fogging; aquatic mosquito egg control and stagnant water inspections, which help keep the mosquito population under control. Here, this program has a multi-million dollar budget. Whether you agree with spraying or not, with all the fresh water we have, mosquitoes are a serious threat, almost year round. Sentinel chickens are tested for Equine Encephalitis, St. Louis encephalitis and West Nile Virus on a regular basis. Almost every year several people still die from one or the other of these diseases, and encephalitis strains are responsible for a number of horse deaths, some years more deaths than from any other air born vector. Mosquitoes also give heartworms to unvaccinated dogs.

You may be wondering what my point is. In 2010 there was an election for Mosquito Control Commissioner and a number of candidates ran. One of them was a young lady we liked very much. She had eye catching pink signs that had pictures of her pretty face on them along with the other campaign info.

Each spring, because Tampa is the home of Yankee Spring Training camp, we get all kinds of visitors associated with the New York Yankees. Tourists, team officials and sportswriters come from all over. One morning I looked up the young lady's name and saw an article written by a New York sportswriter with a title something like, "Candidate Seeks War with Mosquitoes." He went on to ask what mosquitoes could have ever done to her that she would want to eliminate them. She was one of six candidates. I guess he hadn't noticed the other candidate's signs because hers were so striking. I'm sure he thought it was tongue and cheek amusing, but I wasn't amused. Sir, I don't make comments about the way people choose to do things in other places, I think that's bad manners. I don't make judgments about spraying for bed bugs in New York, which are not, so far as I know fatal, so perhaps you shouldn't make jokes about something that can be.

My New Best Friend

The original Little Orphan Peep was so quick and wily that I never got closer than three feet from her while she was growing up. Undoubtedly, her lack of trust helped her to survive all the nights alone until she was old enough to attach herself to the Chanel sister - Spanish Rooster family. She is as bold as they are now. If I sit on the porch they'll walk up the stairs and stare at me like I'm insufficiently caring. Why don't I just hop right up to get them a snack? Lots of the chickens use the porch as a shortcut across the yard. The porch, which is really an 8 x 40 foot deck, has a dowel trimmed rail where the dowels are far enough apart that they just hop up on the porch walk across and hop down rather than walk a few extra feet.

Orphan Peep II was finally secured, or so we thought. My husband picked her up just as she'd gone to sleep and put her in the chicken house with the other chicks her age. We open the door every morning so they can walk around the yard and she was fine. We don't know how she did it because she wasn't small enough to poke through the fence and she was surely too young to fly out, but, there she was back cruising her part of the back yard just like the day before. We thought we were seeing an optical illusion or at

least another chick. She'd acted so forlorn pacing around all alone and staring into the little yard that she'd outgrown, we thought she missed her nest mates, but, obviously being back with her group didn't satisfy her.

If I walk like a duck and talk like a duck?

It had been a little under two months between the time OP II had hopped out of the traveling crate and her recapture and return to her nest mates. After that amount of time, she seems to have forgotten the other chicks she'd spent her first six weeks with. Maybe the reason she always slept between the two little yards was that she was nostalgic for the place instead of the company. Maybe she just liked the two little ducklings that lived there.

There were two little yards with just a few inches of space between them. We move them every few days to give them clean ground to scratch. It's a pretty safe spot. She went right back to visiting with the ducks off and on all day and sleeping right beside them in the little space at night. She's probably just lonely, so why didn't she just stay in the chicken yard with the other peeps?

Unlike her predecessor there's no shyness in her. She's never scooted away like she's frightened of getting caught, even after she was caught. Something about the experience of being caught and returned to her nest mates made her even less shy. Maybe, she's just hungry and has seen the family of four who quickly pace up and down the rail glancing back at the kitchen door in expectation of immediate gratification. I call it Pavlov's Chicken response. She's a pretty smart little peep, because she seems to know that showing up when they do would just get her chased away by the bigger birds. She drops by when she sees me on the porch, but a little bit earlier than they do. She appears to be quite smart for a chicken for she comes at least one hour earlier than the foursome.

Her behavior brings into question the old nature versus nurture question. Does she come to ask for food because she's seen the other chickens receive food, or is she genetically programmed to be food aggressive? When you look at them closely, most hens have similar facial features within breeds.

The Chanel 5 sisters had the long beaks, flat heads and small forward looking eyes of game hens. They had more the appearance of being a game breed that's been raised domestically rather than more fully domestic breed.

Little Orphan Peep will walk right up to me when I'm sitting on the porch. As I've said, most of the chickens and turkeys go over the porch as a shortcut, but, they completely ignore me and don't stop to ask for food.

Only two of our current hens are what I would call, "food aggressive," Original Crow chicken was the same. With each of them, this is a learned rather than a natural behavior. Crow came by it following me as I fed the dogs.

I had a container of dry food in the shed and I also used the stew beef canned food. I fed morning and evening and, at first, she would follow me, hoping I would throw her some dry food. Ducks and turkeys will beg for dry food the same way, because I've never seen poultry who didn't love dry dog food.

In Crow's case giving her an inch encouraged her to demand a mile. When I would open a can she would hop up and if I didn't give her at least one piece of the stew beef, she would just grab it out of the can, or if I didn't move fast enough, peck my finger to get it.

Diversion didn't work for long. I'd sprinkle dry food or corn on the ground and for a couple of days it distracted her long enough. Then she figured out what I was doing and became food aggressive again. It got so bad that I started preparing the food bowls in the shed or the laundry room to avoid getting attacked.

One evening when I was reading on the porch, I looked to my left and the Chanel sister was sitting on the rail staring intently toward me. I realized then that she, or her remaining sister, had to be the mother of Orphan Peep II. They share the same forward facing eyes which have acquired the talent to stare at me until I give them what they want.

Wilder or Tamer Whatever It Takes

Deer have become so plentiful in the past ten years that we see them every day; all we have to do is go outside. Wild populations grow and decline over time. Drought, flood, predators, roads and housing extending further into wild habitats, any number of factors come into play in the rise and fall of populations of wild animals. Just a few years ago during the late 90's people were commenting on the dearth of deer and their small stature. Over the past ten years, the circle of life has revolved again to bring an abundance of well grown, healthy looking deer.

As we all know from Bambi, female deer aren't much for fighting. The males will sometimes establish their place by head butting and rearing up and flailing their legs at each other though.

Most of the time, no injury occurs during these displays. The effect is more like the choreographed rumbles between the Jets and the Sharks at the beginning of *West Side Story*, a show of strength and menace meant to thrill the onlookers and establish hierarchy, rather than inflict real violence.

Whenever youthful hijinx occur, things will sometimes get out of hand. This spring we had a small herd of deer that would show up every evening to glean some evening corn. As often happens, the closer you are to coming onto or leaving the designated deer hunting season the deer will adjust their level of wariness accordingly.

True Spring is far enough away from hunting season that deer shed some of their natural flight response and become quite relaxed among people they're accustomed to seeing on a regular basis. This was just coming out of the biggest acorn winter we'd had in years, so it was a pleasant surprise when we saw so many so soon.

We went for nearly two months without seeing any deer at all. It would have been troubling if we weren't aware of the reason, but, we

knew that once the wild life had exhausted the year's crop of acorns, we'd be seeing them again. We just didn't figure on seeing them so soon.

They returned with a wary game plan. Often when deer wish to find out if a field is a safe place to graze, they send one or more does out as scouts since there is no doe season and somehow they seem to know this. That's why they feel safe to hide behind the ladies. While they hang back and scope out the safety of the situation, the does are usually happy to go out first, since the slower and more timid the men folk are, the more food there is for them to eat first.

This particular group would send out one or two does, then two spikes, which are male deer which haven't formed any branches on their antlers. Spikes are what they're called. After the spikes came, the more mature males come into the field in reverse order of stature. Two points, four points, six points and then the big shots, if there are any. The largest rack in this group was a six pointer and he would always come in last. They were stopping every few steps to make sure I wasn't making the kind of sudden movements that might mean I had a gun.

We have some chairs out back where there's a good view and often in the spring they would be as close as thirty feet away and as long as we didn't make any loud noises like sneezing, or big movements, they were oblivious to us. Sneezing is the sound they make to warn each other of danger. Sneezing and coughing appear. to be the only sounds they make. It appears to be the loudest sound they are capable of.

There's a facility to our northwest that does salvage type work, we don't really see it because we have trees between the two properties. It's a pretty big operation and for a time that spring they worked well into the evening and we would often hear backup warning beeps from the heavy equipment.

This was a chance to observe operant conditioning. The first time the deer were grazing and heard the sound, they looked up jerked their heads toward the sound and then towards me, as if it was my fault. They conferred very briefly and took off.

They lingered at the edge of the woods for about twenty minutes until the unfamiliar sounds subsided. The does and younger bucks came back to graze, but the older boys grazed as close to tree cover as they could and didn't come back any further.

They became accustomed to the sound over a period of about three weeks. That's when they no longer gave the sound any heed at all. They will still often be startled into a temporary retreat by a sudden rooster's crowing or the call of an owl.

I'm a Doe, not a Pushover.

From time to time, food is scarce, particularly in the winter. When trees are bare, grass is dead and seeds are dormant, some animals get very hungry. Often, in a place like Florida this is when deer will do the most damage. They eat roses and other tasty plants that don't lose their leaves.

A couple of years ago we borrowed a night vision camera and mounted it in a tree on a part of the property we call the park, or the field. It's about an acre and a half of grass with three huge old oaks, a tall cabbage palm and one huge twisted old native pine. We'd tried fencing about a twenty foot area and planting peas in the spot one fall. We rolled the fence wire up after they were ready so the deer could eat them, but, the way the deer were attracted to the spot, something was still growing there months after the peas were gone. We started putting out corn in hopes of getting some nice pictures of the deer.

We put the corn out fairly late most days so the chickens would be closer to the house and not see it. Then the wild animals would have a better chance at it.

When we got the film developed we had some excellent shots. There was an especially nice one of a male with antlers standing next

to a wild turkey, one with a pig in the mix and one shot which was a complete surprise.

It's a great picture. It's a shot of two deer rearing up in the traditional fight pose. The one on the left is a fine looking six point buck, but the other one was a complete surprise. The one on the left is a doe. She was doing everything she could to keep that corn for herself.

One of the reasons for the deer's resurgence is probably the bad economy. It's bad for people, but it leaves more fields and woods free of buildings, so they may have a bigger and more varied habitat. There's also quite a bit of land in this county that's protected by the state or the county. There are also large ranches and other land lying undeveloped with hayfields and cows to help claim low green belt tax rates.

Since the late 90's, like much of America, the taxable value of Pasco county land surged, for a while. From 1998 for almost the next ten years it surged from twelve billion in taxable value to thirty eight billion and then went down after the collapse to around eighteen billion around 2009. The veneer of prosperity is still intact, unless you look too close. I'm not sure things have bottomed out yet. It's bad for pets that often are abandoned or taken to shelters in times like these. Sometimes though, it can be good for the wild animals as there's less property development.

One Antler

bout a month ago we noticed that one of the young bucks who'd been a group scout last spring had experienced some sort of mishap. He had one good pointed antler on one side and on the other, there was nothing. It hasn't seemed to hurt his standing in the deer community, for I've seen him with different segments of his original group and nothing seems amiss.

Since deer shed off their antlers each winter, he has as much chance as any other buck to have a great and impressive rack next fall. Two twin bucks can have completely different sized antlers. It all depends on dominance; the food supply and general health. Those are just some of the factors that come into play in determining how big a buck's antlers will grow.

If one gets sick, or has trouble finding enough food, even a buck that has a large impressive rack one year may only grow a small one the next. Sometimes deer who are hit by cars are examined and though they have giant stumps capable of supporting a rack of eight points or more, they will only show a spike. This usually happens to deer that have been through some kind of stress, or illness.

We don't know how he lost his antler. He could have knocked it off on a tree, or while kicking up his heels with the other boys. It will be hard to tell who he is next spring. His youth and boldness make me apprehensive for his chances of surviving hunting season because he is almost as bold about day grazing as a doe. He can be spotted between the woods and the back garden almost any time of day, some days.

A while ago my husband came inside about six in the evening, fuming at something he'd seen. Five of the deer were out by the tower stripping the leaves off the Pummelo grapefruit trees. We can't fence everything. So, we figured hopefully they'd find some other snack soon, because the grapefruit were almost ripe and pulling and tugging on the leaves might cause them to fall. They're never going to be as big as they used to be because fertilizer that was $4.50 a bag in the 90's is now $13.00 and that's a price per ton.

Update: We had to wave a white flag on this issue; the deer had become so destructive that we put an acre of electric fence around the section that held the most productive trees.

The Odd Couple

As I have mentioned, Mr. Orpington and his half Aracuana hen live with White Ears the goat. Most days it seems that the hen is the third wheel on a playful date between two lovers.

We tried for more than a year to see there was a sitting hen with Mr. Orpington, I admit out of vanity and a love of beauty. We wanted him to be content enough to stay in the fence, not get killed and to make some good looking copies of himself. With a hen, at least he might have babies that would inherit his good looks. We thought it would be nice to temper his size and aggression with a more placid disposition while still carrying forward his beauty.

White Ears is over ten years old, she's a tough nanny goat, though she still maintains the good looks of her youth. Even though there are two shelter houses, they are on the wild, wooded side of the

property. Goats are tough, too tough. If you introduce just one male goat into a group of females, you're likely to have a goat population explosion. This is what happened to us for a while.

Back in 2002, my husband and daughter decided goat milk was just what we needed for good health. We had a fence built, with an outer fence with two entry gates into it. This is necessary, for the goat's safety, because they can be escape artists. There is tree shade from the front of the pen in the morning and from the back in the early evening and approximately 80 x 100 feet of interior space. It's a safe space for goats and roosters, not so much for sitting hens. The outer barrier fence on the west side will grow up in dog fennels and other tall weeds, which apparently makes a convenient hiding place for snakes and other predators who will target vulnerable nests and sitting hens.

We originally bought four female goats in 2002. They were sweet natured and easy to handle. They would let you go into the pen and pet them or brush them and were affectionate and appreciative of attention. Unfortunately, to have a regular source of milk you will eventually need a male goat and baby goats. That's where the problems began.

For all their sweet dispositions, goats are the fussiest eaters on the planet. Those stereotypes of goats eating anything and everything, I can say from experience are absolutely not true. The stereotype of goats eating tin cans probably came from one eating the paper label off the can. Goats are extremely picky eaters and will take time and trouble to switch from whatever their preferred feed is to another one. They enjoy nibbling certain types of foliage you can provide for them, but they like to pick and choose. These girls liked oak branches and hibiscus branches and palm fronds, some types of fruit and vegetables, commercial feed, and very little else. Even though they had a lovely small pasture, they seldom ate grass. They're choosy. They like banana peels, but not the fruit, and would nibble apples, but again, not eat the whole fruit. On the whole, they just nibble and waste, at least in my experience.

More Goats, More problems

No male, no milk. Once we introduced a male into the peaceful girly goat foursome, the peace ended. We bought a fine looking Billy goat, just like the ones in the story, *The Three Billy Goats Gruff*. He was a handsome fellow, but, since we acquired him when he was already an adolescent, he was already too aggressive and she goat protective for us to develop an affectionate relationship with.

He was fun to watch though, as he had, for the first time in a long time, plenty of room to run and kick up his heels. He also had four pretty she goats to chase and breed. Soon, there were baby goats and plenty of extra milk. It's pleasant to see goats grazing. They're sweet and exceptionally playful and there are few things cuter than baby goats frolicking. They leap and run around with playful abandon. There was one problem. It was no longer particularly safe to go in and milk White Ears and the other girls. We did it anyway, but, it was kind of scary.

The bonus, at first, was baby goats and the good milk. When two of the babies became young males, dad became competitive and then aggressive. He was a good looking Billy goat, so it wasn't hard finding another home for him.

Just like chickens, goats don't care if the object of their affection is a blood relative, an aunt or even a mother. After another two years, we were in the midst of a population explosion. Eventually there were sixteen of them in the pen and the feed bills were through the roof.

I had never eaten goat before. It had been present at a couple of barbecues I'd been to, but I'd never tried it. We took the broke persons way out, we sold a couple of the males at the livestock auction up in Darby and began killing and butchering a few of the rest. We wouldn't harm the original girls though. Goat meat is actually

pretty good, especially barbecued or used in stews. I spent most of my childhood in the city, so, I'm sometimes conflicted about eating animals I primarily thought of as friends and companions.

Fast forward a couple of more years and two of the original four girls passed away. One succumbed to an infection and the other died from the complications of a breached birth. There were still two original sisters and White Ears toddler son. Within another two years White Ears sister and her son were both dead as well. We tried several times to find a companion animal to entertain White Ears, but rabbits either escaped or were eaten and most of the other poultry we put in the pasture quickly flew out of the fence and away.

When Mr. Orpington became too big and fractious to stay around the other roosters. We gave him a try, not expecting much from the experiment. He was a hit. Not only did he and White Ears get along, they became best friends and seem to share a peculiar, and what appears to be from a human perspective, distinctly physical attraction. He rides around on her back all the time. They also playfully chase at each other and sometimes he will fly up in her face and she will charge back at him.

While we've made several attempts to let him out on furlough as he's aged over the years, he always comes back to her after a few hours. We've given up any hope of him ever having babies that will live long enough to replace him, so we are trying to replace his beauty with some hatchlings we bought from Murray MacMurry Hatchery.

White Ears always had chicken visitors. There's an old orange grove irrigation pipeline from the pump, behind the goat pen. It's used to fill up the fishing hole. This is a system of eight foot long metal pipes which can be clamped together or made to go at angles by using elbows. In dry weather, tasty green grass grows in the shade of the pipes, where the joints come together and there's a little bit of a drip. This draws chickens that are always looking for a nice shady spot to graze and scratch for bugs. They often do us a service with their grass scratching, because if weeds were to grow up around the pipe, they would have to be sprayed with herbicide. Water moccasins love tall weeds, especially if they're in a moist and shady area.

The pipe and some chicken's tendency to find corn wherever you put it, even behind a fence, caused some of the wilier birds to hop the double fence and make a raid on White Ear's feed bin. She would come charging up to scare them off, but she never hurt anyone. She'd always enjoyed trotting up and down watching the chickens grazing on the other side of the fence, or Boomer or Clint out for a walk.

When we put Mr. Orpington into White Ear's pasture we knew he would have to have at least one hen with him, or he'd be compelled to seek females on the outside. His hen would lay and sit and then show back up when the eggs were taken or the chicks were killed. This happened for a while, but she stayed alive and we could hear or see her on a regular basis when we went in and checked on her or brought feed when we saw her off the nest. The last time she hatched out some chicks, we should have gone and gotten them, but she was hiding them in some grass and gave every inclination that she would make us chase about all day trying to take them from her. Tall grasses and weeds are another scary place as you can't see the snakes hiding in them. We should have made more of an effort, because after about a little over a week of successful survival, all three vanished without explanation.

Mr. Orpington was content to stay within the boundaries of his goat fence, most of the time. After a few weeks of non hen companionship, he became restless and the fight between him and Duck ensued. We had to get him another hen, but a setting hen and her progeny would be in danger, so we needed to make sure we had a non setting hen for a future wife/companion for him.

Luckily roosters don't choose hens for their good looks. Beauty seems completely irrelevant to them. Finding a pretty hen wasn't the problem. Finding one that laid eggs without sitting on them and would be content to stay was. The plan was to keep two hens with him, since he'd have had at least that many if he was on the outside. Three different hens that had bantam bloodlines, which meant could fly, left after a few days. A part Aracuana hen that had golden brown feathers tipped in black stayed. She has the typical long neck and forward pitched posture of her ancestors and like them, no rump. She seems content to be queen chicken of her little world, for, due to her Aracuana forebears, she would never have been able to achieve high status in a flock. She eats her corn and lays her eggs and mostly stays out of the way of the Odd Couple.

I call White Ears and Mr. Orpington the odd couple. They frolic about like two best pals on a playground. She occasionally will leap like a very young goat playing and show more happiness than she has in years. In the last two years she hadn't paid as much attention to her own sister. They also graze and eat with the hen. When he hops up on White Ears back when she's grazing, she could buck him off very easily, but, she doesn't.

Unintended Consequences

We all want to save energy. Some people merely want to save money and some want to reduce their carbon footprint out of a sense of responsibility. Ethanol has been an unfortunate side trip leading nowhere on the road to energy independence, in my opinion. It's not rocket science to observe the obvious. Buying corn at artificially high prices, is nothing but a government subsidy to the corn producing states, especially Iowa, for obvious reasons.

In the long run it takes far more energy to produce and transport ethanol than it saves. We all know it and any mechanic can tell you it causes damage to car engines. It's also no secret that rapidly developing parts of the world are demanding more meat in their diet and, aside from chickens and goats, which can forage and rabbits which can be fed many kinds of vegetation, meat production requires feed as well.

Even if you disagree with meat eating or factory farming, artificially inflating the price of corn has cruel unintended consequences. Most of the world uses either corn or rice as the staple of their diet and many of these people are poor, bitterly poor. When a food crop that people eat to stay alive is diverted to Ethanol production, it just seems immoral to me. I dislike preaching, but, in economic times like these, I think we should just put a stop to it.

The other consequence of Ethanol production is to the animals. Usually people who raise a few farm animals can adjust to normal, gradual price increases or the occasional price fluctuations caused by

crop failures. When there's a perfect storm of price increases, crop fluctuations and a whole lot of unemployment and bad economic news, animals are among the first to be affected. Feed stores are even being charged fuel surcharges of up to four hundred dollars a shipment and are having to scramble for ways to bring the feed to their stores at a lower price. Feed prices have skyrocketed in recent years. Pet food prices, especially those which have grain ingredients have gone up also. This has led to millions of dogs, cats and horses being abandoned or put down.

Florida has herds of wild horses people have turned loose in state parks. The feral cat population has also exploded.

Aside from using whatever salvage foods and leftovers we can, we have also let the field grass grow a week or two longer and used it for hay and raked the other side of the road when the landscapers mow the church. We have planted clover and while we don't have enough for more than a seasonal treat, a varied healthy diet is something rabbits especially seem to like. We still have to buy feed, but at least we've been able to curb some of the cost.

Where O Where is Little Orphan Peep

The happy foursome of Spanish rooster, the red Chanel 5 sister, Crow chicken and Little Orphan Peep, with their dogged follower Shadow rooster continued for about six weeks. Abruptly as young kids who aren't ready to settle down will often do, Little Orphan Peep decided to sow some wild oats.

First she showed up in the flock of a young Turken rooster about a year older than she was, who has four devoted hens and three or four more that come and go.

Hens, for all the grief they take being chased and harassed by roosters, are not captives or slaves. Except for the unavoidable task of laying eggs, they can do as they choose. They are free to join a rooster's flock, come and go from different flocks, stay with a group of hens, or be loners like some of the boys. That doesn't mean that they won't be chased and maybe caught by roosters, it just means their living arrangements are a complex set of choices determined perhaps by instinct, perhaps by taste.

Often about eight in the morning when the sun is still on the other side of the palms and pines, you can see most all of the chickens, turkeys and ducks in the same spot. When they're all together you wouldn't know they were a number of individuals and small groups, you'd think they were all one big happy family.

Little Orphan was all grown up and though she was no bigger than a very small bantam, Shadow the rooster seemed smitten with her. While she was with the Turken clan, he switched his shadowing from the Spanish-Crow family to her new group. Clearly his interest was in her not the other two hens in the family, or participating in a blood rivalry with the male. After a few days, she drifted back to her old family. She still wasn't ready to settle down, for a few days later she vanished and popped up with Shadow. They looked nice together, but, out of sync, due to the difference in their size. The Spanish is a small rooster, not as small as some of the bantams, but not large. The Turken is not full blooded and as his mother is small, he's small too. Shadow's not as large as the Leghorn's he looks like, but, he still towers over her. After a few days, she left him too, and returned to her original rooster. There seemed to be no hard feelings and then she disappeared.

A few days later, she wasn't with them. I didn't think much of it after her recent adventures. I saw her with her group around noon the next day. After that she disappeared again. It's her first nest and she seems as if she will be a devoted and steady nester. I can't wait to see who the chicks look like.

The Owls

I must confess I admire owls. I admire their style and skill. Even when they wiped out our goldfish and sit in the trees to view the vulnerable below, I still love to watch them. Owl is my answer to the old question, "What kind of wild animal would you want to be?"

About six months after we moved here, while all the pine trees were still intact, I spotted a slow moving lump of feathers on the ground out by the field. It was an owl. He was injured and wouldn't have lasted long on the ground. He didn't seem frightened, so I went and got my husband and we shooed him into a portable dog crate. We took him to a kindly vet we know and he was fine within a short time.

Not every vet will treat wounded animals gratis and not every vet is qualified to work on birds. You should never just scoop up a wild animal if they are hurt. They can be sick, or lash out because they're hurt or frightened. It's probably best to call whoever the wildlife management authorities are in your area. This time it worked out well, next time I might get hurt. I think if there's a next time, I'll just make the call.

Like other wildlife, sometimes we see a fair amount of owls in the evening and sometimes, weeks or even months go by, when we don't even hear them. As some of the pine trees began to die or be cut a few years after we moved here, the chickens loved to hop up on the stumps. The trees would tend to break off three to four feet off the ground and when we cut them we mimicked nature by taking them off at the same height. This at least allows the stump to rot naturally, though I have to pick them up once they rot to the ground. They provide tasty bugs for the birds and owls like them too.

As some of the pines died, it did open up our view of the forest. Three years ago it must have been the Year of the Owl for we saw more owls in one season than we ever have before or since. They would sit in the trees and then hop down onto the stumps. Once, we saw an owl take off from the top of a pine tree, hop to the stump and then swoop down and catch a young snake, about a foot long.

We often saw them swoop down and snatch up some unknown small creature, probably a lizard or a mouse. It's a curious thing about our little corner of the world, 90% of the owls we see are what are called Big Horned owls, *Bubo Virginianus.* Barn owls are much more common though, in overall numbers. We also have some little owls that burrow in abandoned gopher holes and hollow trees, but around here, Big Horned owls are the ones we most often see. When there were still a couple of tall healthy pines about twenty feet from our chairs, a handsome big owl would sometimes perch in one for a few minutes in the evening. He would sometimes face the woods straight

ahead of us and then turn back to us a full 180 degrees, looking at us as if we were ruining his evening. They've been known to stay up there and eyeball Duck or Mr. White, even though they're rather large for an owl dinner.

In the summer when the evenings are long, we're sometimes surprised by how late it is when we come inside. We'll have a drink or two and it seems like there's always something to look at. We like some television, reading and dancing, but, sometimes nothing can compete with the greatest show on earth.

As the sun goes down over the forest, our birds toddle off to bed and the squirrels and songbirds poach a little corn before dark. It makes for a one of a kind show. The deer will drift through while a few straggler turkeys hurry off to their roosts. As the shift changes, the night creatures come out and the day creatures go off duty and head to the safest places they can find to rest.

We'll sit outside and watch the moon and stars come up, sipping our drinks. I like to make what I call a Redneck wine cooler, sparkling wine mixed with club soda or a cold drink. I like Fresca. Sometimes we're surprised at how late it is when we finally drift back indoors.

A Scream in the Night

For the past twenty years or so, the semi- tropical weather patterns so predictable in the 1960's and 70's have become completely unpredictable. Back then we had a rainy season that normally lasted from mid- June through September and occasional rainfall the rest of the year. Now, in our little corner of Pasco County, we can go nine months or more without rain and except for the hurricanes, our rainfall has been extremely low in probably fifteen of the last twenty years. 2012 was an anomaly year, because for few weeks it rained and then we were underwater.

This kind of weather is not just unpleasant, it's dangerous. Whenever the creek overruns its' banks, habitat and hunting territories are temporarily moved and predators who normally hunt deep in the Preserve are compelled to widen their hunting grounds, or starve. In the long term there's an upside for some animals. Chickens love to hunt for bugs in the field because the rain brings a bumper crop. Sometimes, wading birds have a hard time finding fish along the creek bank while it's rushing, but, they know it will recede quickly and the fish and bugs will be better than ever. In the shorter term small "flood puddles" also form where fish and minnows are washed into them and trapped.

We saw a giant blue heron along the edge of the creek one day. What appeared to be the same bird was in the same spot the next day. When my husband walked out to the edge of the water, he found the bird's prey. There were twenty four large snail shells in a pile next to where the bird was fishing. He was obviously a clever bird, for low water makes for easy pickings, but it takes a clever bird to make the most of a flood.

In over ten years living next to a fairly large patch of wilderness, things have gotten a little safer for the animals on our property, but not as much as we would like. We've gotten better at protecting them and we've let them mix to combine and make smarter, smaller quicker hybrids rather than their big domesticated forebears, but, we can't control the weather. We wish we could for it causes lots of tragedy for people and often for animals as well. Every time we have significantly high rainfall and the creek overflows, chickens get killed by predators who may have never known they existed if it hadn't rained so much.

Around ten one night after the umpteenth day of rain, I was sitting on the porch looking at the clouds roll across the sky. To the north, where Mr. and Mrs. Orpington live with White Ears, I heard the unmistakable squawk of a chicken in distress. It sounded like the hen. There was about forty to sixty seconds of squawking with what sounded like a slight or slightly muffled crow towards the end of the squawk. There was no way to get out there through the puddles and mud in the dark without breaking our necks, so, we just had to wait until morning to see what happened.

As it turned light the next morning, there was Mr. Orpington marching up and down the fence crowing. This in itself seemed odd because roosters often come to the fence to crow at him and challenge him as he is behind the safety of a fence. He seldom pays attention to them though. It looked like his Mrs. was missing. I scouted around the edge of the fences to see if I could find anything suspicious like a pile of feathers.

My appearance at the fence spiked White Ears interest for she thought I'd brought snacks. From one of the two sheds out trotted out Mrs. Hen right behind her. No other chicken except Pretty Hen and her new best friend a tiny crow chicken roost to our north. They all roost in the giant oak or in the chicken house. Was someone stranded down there after a late bug hunt in the puddles and forced to roost in the big oak by the goat pen? Could it have been one of the rooster's who trot up and down with Mr. Orpy having crowing contests that had been trapped by the little pasture and decided to roost in a new spot because the rain caught him unawares? It's a mystery, for no one appeared to be missing. I hope it was just a near miss on the couple that lives with White Ears, but, perhaps I'll never know.

Feisty Turkey Hen

The twenty Royal Palm turkeys we got several years ago contained one surprise. We had accidently gotten a bonus for there was one extra turkey chick, but, she wasn't a Royal Palm. She was a Brown Turkey and from the start she was as much a sister to the other girls as if she was Royal Palm herself. As their numbers dwindled there were three hens left, Fainting Hen, one other Royal Palm and she who came to be known as Feisty Hen.

Feisty Hen had the slight build and soft whispering language of turkey hens. One of the endearing things about turkeys is that they will talk to you. This is probably where the expression, "talk turkey," came from. The Toms will gobble back at you instantly if you gobble at them first. The hen's soft muffled gobble is harder to mimic, but, sometimes they will reward you with turkey conversation of a softer sort.

The three hens would often walk around and feed together. The brown hen would also strike out by herself, from time to time. She was more adventurous than the other ladies, showing bravery and initiative poking around under bushes and dead tree stumps. Unlike her meek sisters who politely retreated from crowds that gathered around corn or vegetables, she would bravely defend what she thought was hers.

During watermelon season the rinds are the most anticipated delicacy among turkeys, chickens, ducks and rabbits. Often we'll finish up a watermelon for breakfast or cut it up to eat later and put the rinds out in the back. Most of the animals aren't close by early, that's when they make their rounds or go graze out by the field, by the grapefruit trees, or over by the shed. When they get back, if no one has beaten them to it there's a treat waiting. Watermelons are almost always a truce zone for the poultry. A fair number of heads can fit inside a watermelon and they most often manage to share pretty well.

Feisty Hen decided one morning that the watermelon was her personal property. As the chickens filtered back from their morning excursions and came toward the watermelon, she charged them and ran them off. Her problem was that she couldn't eat and charge the chickens at the same time. She calmed down and decided to share, for the moment.

In the next few weeks summer tomatoes and peppers got ripe and I've mentioned how much turkeys love tomatoes. There were a lot of cherry tomatoes so I planted them all around other bushes in the back garden thinking the turkeys would enjoy them and we would enjoy watching them chase each other about. If one turkey found some before the others, they would give chase. They looked like a bunch of kids playing tag.

Feisty is just no fun sometimes. Rather than engage in tomato tag with the others she would take position by one of the bushes and dare the Toms to come after the fruits of her harvest. She became so brave she would back fully grown roosters off from lettuce or anything else she wanted. She would back off and let them come forward like any meek little turkey hen, then run at them full speed or jump up and flail at them with her feet. Her behavior was totally out of character and the next thing she did was even stranger.

Florida has its' own special breed of wild turkey, the Osceola Wild Turkey, or *Meleagris gallopavo osceola*. They are only found in Florida and their numbers are fairly robust at an estimated eighty to one hundred thousand. There were a lot of wild turkeys passing through at this time. Normally they begin to show up in early spring and we see different family groups at the fish hole or out in the field on average about nine months a year. The boys become quite excited upon the arrival of new hen faces and go out to fan their feathers and show off their colors to a new audience. The wild hens don't seem interested in their style show either, but, they never give up.

The hens will normally visit and graze with their wild cousins though their caution keeps them closer to the edges of the field than the boys will venture. Feisty wasn't constrained by the normal behavior of the other hens. She'd wander out amongst the wild turkeys and mix with the various groups as if she was a member of one of their families. She was almost impossible to distinguish from the wild turkeys. I began to notice that she was more or less identical to them, so I began to look at pictures of the common Brown turkeys, the eastern Brown turkeys and the Osceola Wild turkeys. I had always thought she was a domestic Brown turkey, but, the more I looked at her, the more I was convinced she had found her kin.

She must have felt at home with them because one morning as they drifted away from the field, south into the swampy woods, she went with them. I wish there had been some distinguishing mark on her so I could tell her from the other wild hens. I keep looking for her when wild flocks pass through. I like to think she might be a member of one of the hen and chick groups who only associate with the males occasionally. She never acted like she had much use for the boys.